CW00972176

GORDON McCALLUM
FIELD COTTAGE
THE LANE
VIRGINIA WATER
SURREY
GU25 4BX

THE POETIC BIBLE

Colin Duriez is General Books Editor for Inter-Varsity Press in Leicester. He has written books on C. S. Lewis, J. R. R. Tolkien and the Inklings, and lectured on them in Ireland, the USA, Finland, Spain and Poland, as well as England. He is currently working on a biography of Francis Schaeffer, under whom he studied for a time at L'Abri in Switzerland. He belongs to Leicester Writers' Club and to the Arts Centre Group. He is deeply interested in the relation of Christ to culture, in the role of the imagination in knowledge, and in reading the Bible as literature.

Though born in Derbyshire, Colin's school years were spent in Paulsgrove and Leigh Park, near Portsmouth, the Welsh Rhondda Valleys, and in Kidderminster in the Midlands. After secondary school, he studied at Istanbul University, Turkey, and the University of Ulster, Coleraine, Northern Ireland. Before joining IVP, he worked in publishing, journalism and teaching.

THE POETIC BIBLE

COLLECTED BY
COLIN DURIEZ

Published in Great Britain in 2001 by
Society for Promoting Christian Knowledge
Holy Trinity Church
Marylebone Road
London NW1 4DU

British Library Cataloguing-in-Publication Data

A catalogue record for this book is available from the British Library

ISBN 0–281–05355–3

Typeset by Pioneer Associates, Perthshire
Printed in Great Britain by
Mackays of Chatham

CONTENTS

To
Suzie Kirby

INTRODUCTION

The Poetic Bible is a collection from the last thousand years and more of English verse, a period during which our language has changed dramatically from its early Germanic form to the diversity and innovation of an international tongue. There exists a wealth of poetry throughout this great period that is inspired by the text of the Bible in various ways: sometimes existing as close paraphrase; other times responding more freely to the spirit of the biblical text. Both broad types are represented in the collection. The more free responses range between what is almost exposition or sermon to poems of devotion or meditation, as in the scriptural reflections of Charles Wesley.

Collecting such poetry together creates a remarkable effect – the works of both great and minor poets sit easily together, unified by their common focus upon and necessary humility before the Word of God. As much as possible my selection follows the biblical order from Genesis and the Pentateuch, through the Histories (the period of the Judges, the Kings and the exile), the Wisdom books, the Prophets, the Gospels and Acts, the Letters, to the Book of Revelation – the Apocalypse.

The biblical story, like all good stories, has a beginning, a middle and an end. The pattern of the story includes creation, the fall of humanity, an unfolding plan of salvation, Jesus' incarnation, life, death and resurrection, the birth of the Church, and the future end times. This story and its sequence is a recurrent inspiration for a millennium of biblical poetry. Often the story has focused upon the Church's calendar, with its seasons and pivotal events. We find the great story inspiring the bardic narratives of early English verse, such as *Genesis*, *Exodus*, *Christ* and *Dream of the Rood*. It is also evident in the subjects chosen for the Mystery Plays of York, Wakefield, Chester, Coventry and elsewhere, such as *The Creation of Adam and Eve*, *Cain and Abel*, *Noah's Flood*, *Abraham and Isaac*, *The Woman Taken in Adultery* and *The Resurrection*. The scripts of these plays belong squarely in the same tradition as the poems in this collection. Thus Isaiah has a prophetic prologue in *The Annunciation*, from the Coventry cycle:

> Then shall much mirth and joy increase,
> And the right root in Israel spring,
> That shall bring forth the grain of holiness;
> And out of danger he shall us bring
> Into that region where he is king,
> Which above all other far doth abound;
> And that cruel Satan he shall confound.

The same grand story, in the nineteenth and early twentieth centuries, energized black American preaching, the basis for the poetry of James Weldon Johnson, such as *The Creation*, with which this collection opens.

This millennium of biblical poetry has an impressive continuity, even though of course there is a diversity of theological interpretation, including Roman Catholic, Puritan and Reformed, Anabaptist and Wesleyan. Most striking is an almost universal perception of Christ in all of Scripture, sometimes blatantly so (as in some paraphrases of the Psalms). The collection is made up of the work of writers who usually see a common thread in the entire canon of Scripture as Christ, whether pre-incarnate or made flesh. Relatedly, they tend to bring out the story and imagery of the Bible using the Gospel narratives as the key to its meaning, particularly Christ's nativity, death, resurrection and promise of future return.

The Poetic Bible is very different from a hymnal. This fact is worth pointing out because many of our enduring hymns began life as poems, and some pieces written as hymns stand as poetry. Unlike poems, however, well-sung hymns tend to be moulded and honed like stones on the seashore through use by successive generations of congregations. Thus Charles Wesley's

> Hark! How all the welkin rings
> Glory to the Kings of Kings!

becomes the familiar

> Hark! The herald angels sing
> Glory to the newborn king

My aim in collecting these poems is to take my reader, as I have been taken myself, back to Scripture itself. *The Poetic Bible* is for people of the Book, shedding unique light on its ancient texts. The collection inevitably raises the complex but fascinating question of the character of the Bible's own poetry.

What strikes a modern reader, I think, most of all is that the Bible has no clear demarcation between poetry and prose. The Hebrew in which the Old Testament is written does not, for instance, distinguish them formally (as we do by broken lines, rhyme and the like). The poetic in Scripture has quite subtle characteristics, set out by scholars (such as Tremper Longman) as features like parallelism, heightened imagery and terseness of language. Much of biblical poetry falls into the section of its books I have denoted as the Wisdom Books, but great passages of the Prophets, or even parts of the Histories, are poetic. A separation of the poetic and prosaic, so familiar to a modern reader, is quite alien to a biblical mind-set. This is not to claim that the Bible's historical records are not deliberately accurate, realistic accounts. In fact, the Bible does not employ poetry to document historical events, only to reflect upon them. The Hebrew portrayal of reality had a characteristic concern for actual events as the footprints of God's providential involvement in human life and history.

A divorce between poetry and prose likely enough points to a historical change in consciousness on our part (those of us conditioned by Western rationalism). This change marks a severe impoverishment. The biblical writers, and most writers represented in this collection, share, I think, an older, wiser consciousness. It could perhaps be called a symbolic perception of reality. This is because their daily perception of people, events and things is shaped by their knowledge of biblical history, stories and key images. They look *at* the world and society *through* a biblical frame, which had for them an overwhelming imaginative pull.

The Bible, I think, encourages such a symbolic perception of reality. It begins symbolically with a seven-day creation and the events in the Garden of Eden and ends with the visions of the Book of Revelation. These have their denouement with the Holy City, the New Jerusalem, within which is the Tree of Life introduced in Genesis. The hero of heroes of Scripture is the Lamb that was slain from the creation of the world. In a profound sense, symbols like these are not merely poetic, but solidly real. The Lamb that was slain, for instance, is linked in a myriad ways to actual events in documented history, such as the crucifixion and resurrection of Christ. Most of all, such symbols are linked to events and facts, not in the first place to concepts, even though they provide subject-matter for thought. (The symbol of the Lamb that was slain for instance helps our thinking about the achievement of the cross.) The primary function of biblical images like these is to bring us into contact with significant events in history; selected events in our real space-time;

events of historical importance; events that relate dramatically to *us*. The world was saved at the particular moment when Jesus, on a cross sanctioned by Pontius Pilate, his life-blood dripping away, cried, 'It is finished!' and committed his spirit to the Father who had forsaken him. How long is a moment? A moment of suffering and unimaginable pain might be psychologically very long, even though Jesus died quickly by the standards of the professional executioners. Yet his death on the cross, and the infinite depth of its significance, is the subject of poetry throughout the long history of the English language represented in *The Poetic Bible*, most powerfully perhaps in the beautiful early English *Dream of the Rood* (page 148).

It may have been comparatively recently that we lost an ancient unity between the poetic and the prosaic, the symbolic and the literal. This was certainly the view of C. S. Lewis and his friend J. R. R. Tolkien, two of the most popular Christian writers of our time. In the Bible, to give an example, 'spirit' is equally 'spirit' and 'breath' and 'wind'. Again, the *logos* of the opening of John's Gospel is a profound unity integrating many meanings which we today have to separate out. The same would be true of the early part of the Book of Genesis; the common separation of fact and poetry in reading these chapters is a mistaken reading. It is equally correct to write a thorough commentary on early Genesis (perhaps by an author who is both theologian and scientist) and to create a poem based on the same chapters like James Weldon Johnson's *The Creation*. They belong to the same world of truth.

By saturating ourselves in the Scriptures, as most of the writers in this collection undoubtedly have, a healing of this division in our perception can begin to take place. There can be a restoration of a basic human unity of consciousness. We find this wholesome consciousness far harder than, for instance, a seventeenth-century English, German or Dutch reader of the Bible or perhaps a Scottish Highlander. For this reason C. S. Lewis advocated a diet made up mainly of old books, i.e. books belonging to the period before our modern one. Perhaps today he could have called such writings 'organic books'! The Bible insists, by its very nature, on looking at the natural and human worlds through its multifaceted appeal to our imaginations. It blatantly appeals to our human taste for a story, and to our delight in the poetic, while at the same time satisfying our minds with its explanatory power and impetus to explore intellectually. This is not even to mention the healing peace that the Bible imparts, its salve for our spirits.

Because the selection of poetry ranges over more than a millennium, I have sometimes put explanatory notes at the end of particular poems. Also on occasions I have inserted an accented 'e', to denote a sounded vowel. For a long period, the plural for instance was clearly sounded, as in 'songès' for 'songs'. This emphasizes the importance of sound in poetry – it is meant to be read by the ear as well as the eye (Job 12.11). Indeed, the power of some poetry (e.g. poetry written in dialect, such as the Spiritual) needs reading aloud to be appreciated.

To offer some help for readers there is a brief glossary at the end, providing information on the poets and some of the particularly notable poems, such as John Milton's *Paradise Lost* or the anonymous *Dream of the Rood*.

The origin of this book really lies in my childhood. At the infant school I attended near Portsmouth I first heard and sang John Milton's paraphrase of Psalm 136,

> Let us with a gladsome mind
> Praise the Lord, for he is kind . . .

(found on page 70). It was not until many years later that I read poetry by Milton, or knew that hymn was his, but its beauty stirred a deep longing in me for God. The words and music together (either of which touches me in the same way today, without fail) impressed on me that God deserves praise by his very nature, and that to make such praise imparts gladness. The next stage in the birth of this book was much more recent, as a result of listening to the musical interpretations of several scriptural passages composed by Suzie Kirby. These songs made me consider the whole matter of poetic and artistic interpretations of the Bible, especially after discovering John Bunyan's homely *Scriptural Poems* – several of which are represented in *The Poetic Bible*. His Foreword to that book speaks of his delight in writing his poems, and his hope that writers better than he will take up a similar task. Bunyan's work has been undeservedly neglected. He writes, referring to the poet George Herbert:

> 'Twould be a most delightsome exercise
> Of profit to themselves and others too:
> If what learned Herbert says, hold true,
> A verse may find him, who a sermon flies,
> And turn delight into a sacrifice . . .

The collection gradually took shape, as I scoured the secondhand bookshops of Hay-on-Wye and the University of Leicester library for biblical poetry from the past millennium. Alison Barr of SPCK was immediately attracted by the project when I told her of it. As well as to her, I am indebted to several friends in particular who encouragingly alerted me to various poems or lent me useful books: Susan Gowans, Hazel Medcalf, Bishop Timothy Dudley-Smith (who introduced me to Charles Wesley's poetic scriptural meditations), Suzie Kirby and Norman Fraser (who acquainted me with the writings of Michael Bruce, the 'Gentle Poet of Lochleven', and gave me a copy of *The Scottish Psalmody*). My thanks also to Marie Palmer for typing up many of the poems while in the throes of decorating her house.

Colin Duriez
Clarendon Park, Leicester

THE
PENTATEUCH

(Genesis to Deuteronomy)

OF GOD

(From England's Parnassus)

I am that one, is, was, and aye shall be,
Who create all of nought, as pleaseth me:
I can destroy, I am the great and just,
The fair, the good, the holy one to trust:
Whose strong right hand this world hath set in frame.
I plague my foe, and grant my servants grace,
All those that knowledge me, and all their race.

Anon.
Trans. Thomas Hudson

THE CREATION
(From God's Trombones)

And God stepped out on space,
And he looked around and said:
I'm lonely –
I'll make me a world.

And far as the eye of God could see
Darkness covered everything,
Blacker than a hundred midnights
Down in a cypress swamp.

Then God smiled,
And the light broke,
And the darkness rolled up on one side,
And the light stood shining on the other,
And God said: That's good!

Then God reached out and took the light in his hands,
And God rolled the light around in his hands
Until he made the sun;
And he set that sun a-blazing in the heavens.
And the light that was left from making the sun
God gathered it up in a shining ball
And flung it against the darkness,
Spangling the night with the moon and stars.
Then down between
The darkness and the light
He hurled the world;
And God said: That's good!

Then God himself stepped down –
And the sun was on his right hand,
And the moon was on his left;
The stars were clustered about his head,
And the earth was under his feet.
And God walked, and where he trod
His footsteps hollowed the valleys out
And bulged the mountains up.

Then he stopped and looked and saw
That the earth was hot and barren.
So God stepped over to the edge of the world
And he spat out the seven seas –
He batted his eyes, and the lightnings flashed –
He clapped his hands, and the thunders rolled –
And the waters above the earth came down,
The cooling waters came down.

Then the green grass sprouted,
And the little red flowers blossomed,
The pine tree pointed his finger to the sky,
And the oak spread out his arms,
The lakes cuddled down in the hollows of the ground,
And the rivers ran down to the sea;
And God smiled again,
And the rainbow appeared,
And curled itself around his shoulder.

Then God raised his arm and he waved his hand
Over the sea and over the land,
And he said: Bring forth! Bring forth!
And quicker than God could drop his hand,
Fishes and fowls
And beasts and birds
Swam the rivers and the seas,
Roamed the forests and the woods,
And split the air with their wings.
And God said: That's good!

Then God walked around,
And God looked around
On all that he had made.
He looked at his sun,
And he looked at his moon,
And he looked at his little stars;
He looked on his world
With all its living things,
And God said: I'm lonely still.

Then God sat down –
On the side of a hill where he could think;
By a deep, wide river he sat down;
With his head in his hands,
God thought and thought,
Till he thought: I'll make me a man!

Up from the bed of the river
God scooped the clay;
And by the bank of the river
He kneeled him down;
And there the great God Almighty
Who lit the sun and fixed it in the sky,
Who flung the stars to the most far corner of the night,
Who rounded the earth in the middle of his hand;
This great God,
Like a mammy bending over her baby,
Kneeled down in the dust
Toiling over a lump of clay
Till he shaped it in his own image;

Then into it he blew the breath of life,
And man became a living soul.
Amen. Amen.

James Weldon Johnson (1871–1938)

O GOD WHO BROUGHT THE LIGHT TO BIRTH
(A meditation on Genesis 1–3)

O God who brought the light to birth,
    the moon and all the starry skies,
who set in space the globe of earth
        and made the sun in splendour rise,
            teach us to love the light, we pray,
            and walk as children of the day.

A fertile earth, a sky and sea,
    you filled with creatures great and small,
and fashioned humankind to be
    your own vice-regents over all:
        teach us your fragile world to tend,
        and live as all creation's friend.

Delight and purpose, work and rest,
    and innocence a garden made,
with human love and marriage blest,
    before the flowers began to fade:
        teach us your purpose to fulfil
        and find delight within your will.

What sin was theirs who fell from grace
    enslaved by one forbidden tree,
to found a fallen human race
    no longer unashamed and free:
        teach us to flee from Satan's power
        and keep us in temptation's hour.

For Christ has crushed the serpent's head
    to put an end to griefs and sins;
through him the powers of death are dead
    and resurrection life begins:
        teach us to make his triumphs plain,
        and in him live, and rise, and reign.

Timothy Dudley-Smith (b. 1926)

'LET THERE BE LIGHT'

Thou whose Almighty Word
Chaos and darkness heard,
And took their flight;
Hear us, we humbly pray,
And where the gospel-day
Sheds not its glorious ray,
Let there be light!

Thou, who didst come to bring
On thy redeeming wing
Healing and sight;
Health to the sick in mind,
Sight to the inly blind,
O now to all mankind
Let there be light!

Spirit of truth and love,
Life-giving, holy Dove,
Speed forth thy flight;
Move on the waters' face,
Spreading the beams of grace,
And in earth's darkest place
Let there be light!

Blessed and holy Three,
Glorious Trinity,
Grace, love, and might,
Boundless as ocean's tide,
Rolling in fullest pride,
Through the world far and wide,
Let there be light!

John Marriott (1780–1825)

THE REBELLION AND FALL OF LUCIFER

(From the poem Genesis, lines 1–91)

It is proper and right   that we praise with our lips
And love with our hearts   the Warden of heaven,
The Lord of hosts.   He is Source of all strength,
Of all high creatures   Almighty King!
Never had He birth   nor any beginning;
Nor ever shall His glory   come to an end;
But always for ever   as Ruler He reigns
O'er angelic thrones.   Righteous and just
He held in high splendour   the courts of heaven
Which far and wide   were stablished and founded
By the might of God   for the sons of glory,

The wardens of souls.   The heavenly hosts
Knew joy and delight,   bright bliss with their Lord.
  Great was their glory!   His mighty thanes
Honoured their Prince,   praised Him with gladness
As Lord of life,   had exceeding delight
In their Sovereign's splendour.   They knew no sin
Nor any evil,   but lived in peace
With their Lord for ever.   Naught else they knew
In the heavenly realms   save right and truth,
Till an angel prince   misled through pride
Fell into error.   Then they followed no longer
Their eternal welfare   but turned them away
From love of the Lord.   Loudly they boasted
In their banded strength   they would share with God
His glorious dwelling   spacious and shining.
Evil befell them,   envy and pride
And the angel' s presumption,   he first who sought
To perform this folly,   to wake it and weave it.
Thirsting for battle   he boldly declared
He would build a home   and a high seat
In the northern regions   of the heavenly realm.
  Then God was wrathful,   enraged at the band
He formerly honoured   with grandeur and glory.
He built for those traitors   a wretched abode,
The terrors of hell   and fearful afflictions,
To reward their works;   made ready hell's dungeon,
The bottomless, joyless   abode of pain,
For the angel warden,   the exiled host.
He saw hell spread   in eternal darkness
Fraught with torment   and filled with flame,
With freezing cold,   red fire and smoke;
Dire the pain   He ordained in that prison.
Grimly begotten   their sins against God;
Grim in return   the reward He gave them!
  Savage-hearted   they said they willed
To seize the kingdom,   as they easily could.
But that hope failed them   when Heaven's High-King,
He the Most High   and Monarch of all,
Lifted His hand   against their host.
The fallen angels   foolish and false
Might not prevail   with force against God;
But He bowed their courage   and broke their pride;

In His anger deprived them   of triumph and power,
Of glory and splendour;   despoiled His foes
Of peace and blessing,   of honour and bliss.
By His sovereign strength   on His adversaries
With crushing ruin   He wreaked His wrath.
  His heart was hardened.   Grimly incensed
He grasped the rebels   with hostile grip;
Angry-hearted   He held them and broke them
And took from those traitors   their heavenly thrones.
Our Maker banished   and hurled from heaven
The insolent angels,   the faithless horde.
That hostile host,   those hateful spirits,
The Lord sent forth   on a long, long journey.
Their boasting failed;   their vaunt was broken,
Their force defeated,   their form defiled.
Thereafter those dark souls   dwelt in exile;
They had little cause   to delight in their lot,
But abased in hell-torment   wretched abode
Enduring woe   in the depths of darkness,
Suffering sorely   in sorrow and pain
A gruesome requital,   a grim reward,
Because they began   a strife against God.
  Then was peace once more   and repose in heaven,
Fair customs of concord,   a Leader beloved
By all His thanes,   and a glory growing
For the blissful band   that abode with God.
The citizens of heaven,   the home of glory,
Were once more united.   Dissension ceased,
Struggle and strife   between angel legions,
When the rebel spirits   bereft of light
Were hurled from heaven.   Behind them lay
In God's fair kingdom   far-stretching seats
Filled with abundance   of growing gifts,
Verdant and sunny,   vacant of dwellers,
After the evil angels   were cast into hell
And imprisoned deep   under locks of pain.

Trans. Charles W. Kennedy (1882–1969)

THE MEETING OF ADAM AND EVE

*(Adam is in an unspoiled environment, and has a perfect personal
relationship with the living God, maker of heaven and earth. Yet he is
alone. He asks for an equal for companionship, a suitable helper to stand
beside him. God answers his need. This extract from* Paradise Lost
*celebrates John Milton's high view of the unique companionship of sexual
love within the marriage of free persons.)*

Let not my words offend thee, Heavenly Power,
My Maker, be propitious while I speak.
Hast thou not made me here thy substitute,
And these inferior far beneath me set?
Among unequals what society
Can sort, what harmony or true delight?
Which must be mutual, in proportion due
Given and received; but in disparity
The one intense, the other still remiss
Cannot well suit with either, but soon prove
Tedious alike: Of fellowship I speak
Such as I seek, fit to participate
All rational delight, wherein the brute
Cannot be human consort; they rejoice
Each with their kind, Lion with Lioness;
So fitly them in pairs thou hast combined;
Much less can Bird with Beast, or Fish with Fowl
So well converse, nor with the Ox the Ape;
Worse then can Man with Beast, and least of all.

    Whereto the Almighty answered, not displeased.
A nice and subtle happiness I see
Thou to thy self proposest, in the choice
Of thy Associates, Adam, and wilt taste
No pleasure, though in pleasure, solitary.
What thinkst thou then of me, and this my State,
Seem I to thee sufficiently possessed
Of happiness, or not? who am alone
From all Eternity, for none I know
Second to me or like, equal much less.

How have I then with whom to hold converse
Save with the Creatures which I made, and those
To me inferior, infinite descents
Beneath what other Creatures are to thee?

He ceased, I lowly answered. To attain
The heighth and depth of thy Eternal ways
All human thoughts come short, Supreme of things;
Thou in thy self art perfect, and in thee
Is no deficience found; not so is Man,
But in degree, the cause of his desire
By conversation with his like to help,
Or solace his defects. No need that thou
Shouldst propagate, already infinite;
And through all numbers absolute, though One;
But Man by number is to manifest
His single imperfection, and beget
Like of his like, his Image multiplied,
In unity defective, which requires
Collateral love, and dearest amity.
Thou in thy secrecy although alone,
Best with thy self accompanied, seekest not
Social communication, yet so pleased,
Canst raise thy Creature to what heighth thou wilt
Of Union or Communion, deified;
I by conversing cannot these erect
From prone, nor in their ways complacence find.

Thus I emboldened spake, and freedom used
Permissive, and acceptance found, which gained
This answer from the gracious voice Divine.

Thus far to try thee, Adam, I was pleased,
And find thee knowing not of Beasts alone,
Which thou hast rightly named, but of thy self,
Expressing well the spirit within thee free,
My Image, not imparted to the Brute,
Whose fellowship therefore unmeet for thee
Good reason was thou freely shouldst dislike,
And be so minded still; I, ere thou spakest,
Knew it not good for Man to be alone,
And no such company as then thou sawest

Intended thee, for trial only brought,
To see how thou couldest judge of fit and meet:
What next I bring shall please thee, be assured,
Thy likeness, thy fit help, thy other self,
Thy wish, exactly to thy heart's desire.

    He ended, or I heard no more, for now
My earthly by his Heavenly overpowered,
Which it had long stood under, strained to the heighth
In that celestial Colloquy sublime,
As with an object that excels the sense,
Dazzled and spent, sunk down, and sought repair
Of sleep, which instantly fell on me, called
By Nature as in aid, and closed mine eyes.

Mine eyes he closed, but open left the Cell
Of Fancy my internal sight, by which
Abstract as in a trance methought I saw,
Though sleeping, where I lay, and saw the shape
Still glorious before whom awake I stood;
Who stooping opened my left side, and took
From thence a Rib, with cordial spirits warm,
And Life-blood streaming fresh; wide was the wound,
But suddenly with flesh filled up and healed:
The Rib he formed and fashioned with his hands;
Under his forming hands a Creature grew,
Manlike, but different sex, so lovely faire,
That what seemed fair in all the World, seemed now
Mean, or in her summed up, in her contained
And in her looks, which from that time infused
Sweetness into my heart, unfelt before,
And into all things from her Air inspired
The spirit of love and amorous delight.

She disappeared, and left me dark, I waked
To find her, or for ever to deplore
Her loss, and other pleasures all abjure:
When out of hope, behold her, not far off,
Such as I saw her in my dream, adorned
With what all Earth or Heaven could bestow
To make her amiable: On she came,
Led by her Heavenly Maker, though unseen,

And guided by his voice, nor uninformed
Of nuptial Sanctity and marriage Rites:
Grace was in all her steps, Heaven in her Eye,
In every gesture dignity and love.
I overjoyed could not forbear aloud.

      This turn hath made amends; thou hast fulfilled
Thy words, Creator bounteous and benign,
Giver of all things faire, but fairest this
Of all thy gifts, nor enviest. I now see
Bone of my Bone, Flesh of my Flesh, my Self
Before me; Woman is her Name, of Man
Extracted; for this cause he shall forgo
Father and Mother, and to his Wife adhere;
And they shall be one Flesh, one Heart, one Soul.

      She heard me thus, and though divinely brought,
Yet Innocence and Virgin Modesty,
Her virtue and the conscience of her worth,
That would be wooed, and not unsought be won,
Not obvious, not obtrusive, but retired,
The more desirable, or to say all,
Nature her self, though pure of sinful thought,
Wrought in her so, that seeing me, she turned;
I followed her, she what was Honour knew,
And with obsequious Majesty approved
My pleaded reason. To the Nuptial Bower
I led her blushing like the Morn: all Heaven,
And happy Constellations on that hour
Shed their selectest influence; the Earth
Gave sign of gratulation, and each Hill;
Joyous the Birds; fresh Gales and gentle Aires
Whispered it to the Woods, and from their wings
Flung Rose, flung Odours from the spicy Shrub,
Disporting, till the amorous Bird of Night
Sung Spousal, and bid haste the Evening Star
On his Hill top, to light the bridal Lamp.

Thus I have told thee all my State, and brought
My Story to the sum of earthly bliss
Which I enjoy, and must confess to find

In all things else delight indeed, but such
As used or not, works in the mind no change,
Nor vehement desire, these delicacies
I mean of Taste, Sight, Smell, Herbs, Fruits, and Flowers,
Walks, and the melody of Birds; but here
Far otherwise, transported I behold,
Transported touch; here passion first I felt,
Commotion strange, in all enjoyments else
Superior and unmoved, here only weak
Against the charm of Beauty's powerful glance.
Or Nature failed in me, and left some part
Not proof enough such Object to sustain,
Or from my side subducting, took perhaps
More then enough; at least on her bestowed
Too much of Ornament, in outward show
Elaborate, of inward less exact.

For well I understand in the prime end
Of Nature her the inferior, in the mind
And inward Faculties, which most excel,
In outward also her resembling less
His Image who made both, and less expressing
The character of that Dominion given
O'er other Creatures; yet when I approach
Her loveliness, so absolute she seems
And in her self complete, so well to know
Her own, that what she wills to do or say,
Seems wisest, virtuousest, discreetest, best;
All higher knowledge in her presence falls
Degraded, Wisdom in discourse with her
Looses discountenanced, and like folly shows;
Authority and Reason on her wait,
As one intended first, not after made
Occasionally; and to consummate all,
Greatness of mind and nobleness their seat
Build in her loveliest, and create an awe
About her, as a guard Angelic placed.

John Milton (1608–74)

EDEN IS THAT OLD-FASHIONED HOUSE
(See Genesis 3.23)

Eden is that old-fashioned House
We dwell in every day
Without suspecting our abode
Until we drive away.
How fair on looking back, the Day
We sauntered from the Door –
Unconscious our returning,
But discover it no more.

Emily Dickinson (1830–86)

ADAM LAY IBOUNDEN

Adam lay ibounden,
Bounden in a bond.
Four thousand winter
Thought he not too long.
And all was for an apple,
An apple that he took,
As clerkès finden written
In theirè book.
Ne had the apple taken been,
The apple taken been,
Ne haddè never our Lady
A been heaven's queen.
Blessed be the time
That apple taken was,
Therefore we may singèn
'Deo gracias'.

Anon. (fifteenth century)

ibounden: enchained; **clerkès**: scholars; **a**: have; **Deo gracias**: Thanks be to God.

HE SEEKS HIS RUINED CREATURE
(They heard the voice of the Lord God walking in the garden
in the cool of the day – Genesis 3.8)

Not on the whirlwind's wings he flies,
    Not in the thunder's voice he speaks,
But that the fallen man may rise,
    The Lord his ruined creature seeks:
Not in the burning blaze of day,
    (For fury hath no place in him,)
But placid as the evening ray,
    He comes, to sentence, and redeem.

Charles Wesley (1707–88)

WHAT A TRYIN' TIME

O Adam, where are you?
O what a tryin' time!
Lord, I'm in de Garden,
O what a tryin' time!

Adam, you ate de apple,
O what a tryin' time!
Lord, Eve, she gave it to me,
O what a tryin' time.

Adam, it was forbidden,
O what a tryin' time!
Lord said, 'Walk out de Garden,'
O what a tryin' time!

Traditional Black American Spiritual

THE LATE PASSENGER

The sky was low, the sounding rain was falling dense and dark,
And Noah's Sons were standing at the window of the Ark.

The beasts were in, but Japhet said, 'I see one creature more
Belated and unmated there come knocking at the door.'

'Well let him knock,' said Ham, 'Or let him drown or learn to swim.
We're overcrowded as it is; we've got no room for him.'

'And yet it knocks, how terribly it knocks,' said Shem,
'Its feet are hard as horn – but oh the air that comes from it is sweet.'

'Now hush,' said Ham, 'You'll waken Dad, and once he comes to see
What's at the door, it's sure to mean more work for you and me.'

Noah's voice came roaring from the darkness down below,
'Some animal is knocking. Take it in before we go.'

Ham shouted back, and savagely he nudged the other two,
'That's only Japhet knocking down a brad-nail in his shoe.'

Said Noah, 'Boys, I hear a noise that's like a horse's hoof.'
Said Ham, 'Why, that's the dreadful rain that drums upon the roof.'

Noah tumbled up on deck and out he put his head;
His face went grey, his knees were loosed, he tore his beard and said,

'Look, look! It would not wait. It turns away. It takes its flight.
Fine work you've made of it, my Sons, between you all to-night!

'Even if I could outrun it now, it would not turn again
– Not now. Our great discourtesy has earned its high disdain.

'Oh noble and unmated beast, my Sons were all unkind;
In such a night what stable and what manger will you find?

'Oh golden hoofs, oh cataracts of mane, oh nostrils wide
With indignation! Oh the neck wave-arched, the lovely pride!

'Oh long shall be the furrows ploughed across the hearts of men
Before it comes to stable and to manger once again,

'And dark and crooked all the ways in which our race shall walk,
And shrivelled all their manhood like a flower with broken stalk,

'And all the world, oh Ham, may curse the hour when you were
   born;
Because of you the Ark must sail without the Unicorn.'

C. S. Lewis (1898–1963)

ISAAC AND REBEKAH
(See Genesis 24)

Who is this Man
        that walketh in the field,
O Eleazar,
        steward to my lord?

And Eleazar
        answered her and said,
Daughter of Bethuel,
        it is other none
but my lord Isaac,
        son unto my lord;
Who, as his wont is,
        walketh in the field
in the hour of evening
        meditating there.

Therefore Rebekah
        hasted where she sat,
And from her camel
        lighting to the earth
Sought for a veil,
        and put it on her face.

Wherefore he came,
        and met them on the field
Whom, when Rebekah
        saw, she came before,
Saying, Behold
        the handmaid of my lord,
Who for my lord's sake
        travel from my land.

But he said, O
          thou blessed of our God,
Come, for the tent
          Is eager for thy face.
Shall not thy husband
          be unto thee more than
Hundreds of kinsmen
          living in thy land?

And Eleazar answered,
          Thus and thus,
Even according
          as thy father bade,
Did we; and thus and
          thus it came to pass;
Lo! Is not this
          Rebekah, Bethuel's child?

And as he ended
          Isaac spoke and said,
Surely my heart
          went with you on the way,
When with the beasts
          ye came unto the place.

Truly, O child
          of Nahor, I was there,
When to thy mother
          and thy mother's son
Thou madest answer,
          saying, I will go.
And Isaac brought her
          to his mother's tent.

Arthur Hugh Clough (1819–61)

WRESTLING JACOB
(Genesis 32.24–31)

Come, O thou Traveller unknown,
Whom still I hold, but cannot see!
My company before is gone,
And I am left alone with thee;

With thee all night I mean to stay,
And wrestle till the break of day.

I need not tell thee who I am,
My misery and sin declare;
Thyself hast called me by my name,
Look on thy hands, and read it there;
But who, I ask thee, who art Thou?
Tell me Thy name, and tell me now.

In vain thou strugglest to get free,
I never will unloose my hold!
Art thou the Man that died for me?
The secret of thy love unfold;
Wrestling, I will not let thee go,
Till I thy name, thy nature know.

Wilt thou not yet to me reveal
Thy new, unutterable name?
Tell me, I still beseech thee, tell;
To know it now resolved I am;
Wrestling, I will not let thee go,
Till I thy name, thy nature know.

What though my shrinking flesh complain,
And murmur to contend so long?
I rise superior to my pain,
When I am weak, then I am strong
And when my all of strength shall fail,
I shall with the God-man prevail.

Yield to me now, for I am weak,
But confident in self-despair;
Speak to my heart, in blessings speak,
Be conquered by my instant prayer;
Speak, or thou never hence shalt move,
And tell me if thy name is Love.

'Tis Love! 'tis Love! thou diedst for me!
I hear thy whisper in my heart;
The morning breaks, the shadows flee,
Pure, universal love thou art;

To me, to all, thy bowels move;
Thy nature and thy name is Love.

My prayer hath power with God; the grace
Unspeakable I now receive;
Through faith I see thee face to face,
I see thee face to face, and live!
In vain I have not wept and strove;
Thy nature and thy name is Love.

I know thee, Saviour, who thou art.
Jesus, the feeble sinner's friend;
Nor wilt thou with the night depart.
But stay and love me to the end,
Thy mercies never shall remove;
Thy nature and thy name is Love.

The Sun of righteousness on me
Hath rose with healing in his wings,
Withered my nature's strength; from thee
My soul its life and succour brings;
My help is all laid up above;
Thy nature and thy name is Love.

Contented now upon my thigh
I halt, till life's short journey end;
All helplessness, all weakness, I
On thee alone for strength depend,
Nor have I power from thee to move;
Thy nature and thy name is Love.

Lame as I am, I take the prey,
Hell, earth, and sin, with ease o'ercome;
I leap for joy, pursue my way,
And as a bounding hart fly home,
Through all eternity to prove
Thy nature and thy name is Love.

Charles Wesley

JOSEPH FELL A-DREAMING

Joseph fell a-dreaming.
He dreamed of sheaves of grain;
One stood upright like a tree,
The rest bowed down again.

His dreams came with the night
And he told them in the noon.
He dreamed of the eleven stars,
The sun and the moon.

The sun was his father,
The moon was his mother,
Of all the stars, the brightest star
Was Benjamin his brother.

Eleanor Farjeon (1881–1965)

POTIPHAR'S WIFE
(From The Life of Joseph)

And now these merchants, sons of Ishmael,
Again did poor afflicted Joseph sell,
To an Egyptian, named Potiphar,
The captain of King Pharaoh's men of war.
And God was with him, and did greatly bless,
And crown his undertakings with success.
Whereof his master being well aware,
Committed all he had to Joseph's care;
And made him overseer of his house,
And, from the time his master us'd him thus,
The Lord was pleas'd to give him to partake,
So many blessings, e'en for Joseph's sake:
Of that with plenty he was hedg'd about,
And prospered within door and without.
Such was his master's love, and he so just,
That all things were committed to his trust.

Now Joseph was grown up to manly stature,
Of goodly presence, and most comely feature.

Wherefore his mistress, with a lustful eye,
Beheld his beauty, and resolv'd to try,
If to unchaste embraces she could gain
The youth, but her endeavours prov'd in vain:
For he refus'd, and said, My master knows
In all the house of nothing that he owes,
For his concerns are all at my dispose:
There's not a thing that he hath kept from me
But all is in my hand, save only thee;
Then how can I commit so foul a fact,
And the displeasure of my God contract?
Yet still she sued, and still did he deny her,
Refusing to be with her, or lie by her.

Now on a time when all the men were gone
Out of the house, and she was left alone:
And Joseph at that instant coming in,
About some business he'd to do within;
She took advantage of their being together,
And held his clothes to force him to lie with her.
But Joseph strove, and from her hands got loose,
And left his coat, and fled out of the house.

And when she saw that he had made's escape,
She call'd her servants, and proclaim'd a rape:
Come see now how this Hebrew slave, said she,
Your master's favourite, hath affronted me.
He came to violate my chastity,
And when he heard that I began to cry,
And call for help, afraid lest you should find him,
He's fled, and left his garment here behind him.

And now to give her words the greater credit,
Until her husband's coming home, she hid it,
To whom she spake, and said, Why hast thou brought
This Hebrew here, to set me thus at nought?
The slave attempted to defile my bed,
And when I cry'd, he left his coat and fled,
See here it is. Which when he saw, and heard
The heavy accusation she preferr'd,
He was exceeding wroth at his behaviour,
And utterly cashier'd him from his favour;

Nay more, he cast him into prison, where
In fetters bound, King Pharaoh's pris'ners were.

But Joseph's God, who never yet forsook
Him in extremity, was pleas'd to look
With great compassion on his injuries,
And gave him favour in the keeper's eyes;
So that he was entrusted with the care
And charge of all the pris'ners that were there:
All were committed unto Joseph's hand,
And what was done, was done at his command.
The prison-keeper took no care at all,
Of ought that he entrusted him withal;
Because he saw that God was with him, and
All things did prosper that he took in hand.

John Bunyan (1628–88)

MIRIAM

Hush my mother's infant lusty
hush my fear-born brother nigh
rock you still in paper's cradle
cry you not, or you will die

Rushes taller than your manhood
hide you now from club and sword
neighbours' howls forget, and slumber
on the swaying water-sward

Rose a king who knew not Joseph
feared our numbers, feared our poise
feared our strength within his nation
spoke the killing of our boys

Cunning she who bore you quietly
cunning midwife I must be
cunning now to rock you, rock you
on the river tenderly

Hush, and hear not my heart beating
for the story that's to come
mist-enfolded seeps toward me
in a howl that must be dumb

Silent children, silent women,
silent men and silent bones
silent shoes in piles unnumbered
silent dust among the stones –

Here's the woman with her women
with her barren sorrow bowed
jewels, gold and slaves unnumbered
cannot soothe her field unploughed

Cunning I, my mother's daughter
cannot hush you, but can save
but can lift you from the water
king's son make from son of slave

Running now to fetch my mother
running now to lose the sight
of the silent dust unslumbered
mist-encroaching through my flight

Mother, Mother, run and feed him –
of his origins be dumb –
close your ears against the howling
of the mothers still to come

Alison Leonard (b. 1944)

LET MY PEOPLE GO!

When Israel was in Egypt's land,
Let my people go!
Oppress'd so hard they could not stand,
Let my people go!

Go down, Moses,
'Way down in Egypt's land,
Tell ole Pharaoh,
Let my people go!

'Thus saith the Lord,' bold Moses said,
Let my people go!
If not I'll smite your firstborn dead,
Let my people go!

No more shall they in bondage toil,
Let my people go!
Let them come out with Egypt's spoil,
Let my people go!

Oh, 'twas a dark an' dismal night
Let my people go!
Let them come out with Egypt's spoil,
Let my people go!

Go down, Moses,
'Way down in Egypt's land,
Tell ole Pharaoh,
Let my people go!
Traditional Black American Spiritual

THE WATERS THAT WERE IN THE RIVER TURNED TO BLOOD
(Exodus 7.20)

He turned their water into blood,
    When vengeance was His dread design:
But, thanks to the incarnate God,
    He turned our water into wine!

Charles Wesley

AN ANTE-BELLUM SERMON

We is gathahed hyeah, my brothahs,
    In dis howlin' wildaness,
Fu' to speak some words of comfo't
    to each othah in distress.

An' we chooses fu' ouah subjic'
  Dis – we'll 'splain it by an' by;
'An' de Lawd said, "Moses, Moses,"
  An' de man said, "Hyeah am I." '

Now ole Pher'oh, down in Egypt,
  Was de wuss man evah bo'n,
An' he had de Hebrew chillun
  Down dah wukin' in his co'n;
'Twell de Lawd got tiahed o' his foolin',
  An' sez he: 'I'll let him know –
Look hyeah, Moses, go tell Pher'oh
  Fu' to let dem chillun go.'

'An' ef he refuse to do it,
  I will make him rue de houah,
Fu' I'll empty down on Egypt
  All de vials of my powah.'
Yes, he did – an' Pher'oh's ahmy
  Wasn't wuth a ha'f a dime;
Fu' de Lawd will he'p his chillun,
You kin trust him evah time.

An' yo' enemies may 'sail you
  In de back an' in de front;
But de Lawd is all aroun' you,
  Fu' to ba' de battle's brunt.
Dey kin fo'ge yo' chains an' shackles
  F'om de mountains to de sea;
But de Lawd will sen' some Moses
  Fu' to set his chillun free.

An' de lan' shall hyeah his thundah,
  Lak a blas' f'om Gab'el's ho'n,
Fu' de Lawd of hosts is mighty
  When he girds his ahmor on.
But fu' feah some one mistakes me,
  I will pause right hyeah to say,
Dat I'm still a-preachin' ancient,
  I ain't talkin' 'bout to-day.

But I tell you, fellah christuns,
  Things'll happen mighty strange;
Now, de Lawd done dis fu' Isrul,
  An' his ways don't nevah change,
An' de love he showed to Isrul
  Wasn't all on Isrul spent;
Now don't run an' tell yo' mastahs
  Dat I's preachin' discontent.

'Cause I isn't; I'se a-judgin'
  Bible people by deir ac's;
I'se a-givin' you de Scriptuah,
  I'se a-handin' you de fac's.
Cose ole Pher'oh b'lieved in slav'ry,
  But de Lawd he let him see,
Dat de people he put bref in, –
  Evah mothah's son was free.

An' dah's othahs thinks lak Pher'oh,
  But dey calls de Scriptuah liar,
Fu' de Bible says, 'a servant
  Is a-worthy of his hire.'
An' you cain't git roun' nor thoo dat,
  An' you cain't git ovah it,
Fu' whatevah place you git in,
  Dis hyeah Bible too'll fit.

So you see de Lawd's intention,
  Evah sence de worl' began,
Was dat his almighty freedom
  Should belong to evah man,
But I think it would be bettah,
  Ef I'd pause agin to say,
Dat I'm talkin' 'bout ouah freedom
  In a Bibleistic way.

But de Moses is a-comin',
  An' he's comin' suah and fas':
We kin hyeah his feet a-trompin',
  We kin hyeah his trumpit blas'.

But I want to wa'n you people,
  Don't you git too brigity;
An' don't you git to braggin'
  'Bout dese things, you wait an' see.

But when Moses wif his powah
  Comes an' sets us chillun free,
We will praise de gracious Mastah
  Dat has gin us liberty;
An' we'll shout ouah halleluyahs,
  On dat mighty reck'nin' day,
When we'se reco'nized ez citiz' –
  Huh uh! Chillun, let us pray!

Paul Laurence Dunbar (1872–1906)

THE PILLAR OF CLOUD
(From The Dream of Gerontius)

Lead, Kindly Light, amid the encircling gloom,
    Lead Thou me on!
The night is dark, and I am far from home –
    Lead Thou me on!
Keep Thou my feet; I do not ask to see
The distant scene, – one step enough for me.

I was not ever thus, nor pray'd that Thou
    Should'st lead me on.
I loved to choose and see my path; but now
    Lead Thou me on!
I loved the garish day, and, spite of fears,
Pride ruled my will: remember not past years.

So long Thy power hath blest me, sure it still
    Will lead me on,
O'er moor and fen, o'er crag and torrent, till
    The night is gone;
And with the morn those angel faces smile
Which I have loved long since, and lost awhile.

John Henry Newman (1801–90)

SHADOW AND COOLNESS

Shadow and coolness, Lord, art thou to me;
Cloud of my soul, lead on, I follow thee.
What though the hot winds blow,
Fierce heat beat up below,
Fountains of water flow –
    Praise, praise to thee.

Clearness and glory, Lord, art thou to me;
Light of my soul, lead on, I follow thee.
All through the moonless night,
Making its darkness bright,
Thou art my heavenly light –
    Praise, praise to thee.

Shadow and shine art thou, dear Lord, to me;
Pillar of cloud and fire, I follow thee.
What though the way be long,
In thee my heart is strong,
Thou art my joy, my song –
    Praise, praise to thee.

Amy W. Carmichael (1867–1951)

A PARAPHRASE ON LEVITICUS CHAPTER XI, AFTER THE MANNER OF MASTER GEOFFREY CHAUCER IN HIS *ASSEMBLY OF FOWLS*
(See Leviticus 11.13–19)

Of feathered fowls, that fan the buxom air,
Not all alike were made for food to men;
For, these thou shalt not eat, doth God declare,
Twice ten their number, and their flesh unclean:
First the great eagle, bird of feigned Jove,
Which Thebans worship, and diviners love:

Next ossifrage, and osprey, (both one kind)
Of luxury, and rapine, emblems meet,
That haunt the shores, the choicest prey to find,
And burst the bones, and scoop the marrow sweet:
The vulture, void of delicace, and fear,
Who spareth not the pale dead man to tear:

The tall-built swan, fair type of pride confessed;
The pelican, whose sons are nursed with blood,
Forbid to man! – She stabbeth deep her breast,
Self-murderess through fondness to her brood:
They too that range the thirsty wilds among,
The ostriches, unthoughtful of their young:

The raven ominous, (as Gentiles hold)
What time she croaketh hoarsely *A la Morte*;
The hawk, aerial hunter, swift, and bold,
In feats of mischief trained for disport;
The vocal cuckoo, of the falcon race,
Obscene intruder in her neighbour's place:

The owl demure, who loveth not the light,
(Ill semblance she of wisdom to the Greek)
The smallest fowls' dread foe, the coward kite,
And the still heron, arresting fishes meek
The glutton cormorant, of sullen mood:
Regarding no distinction in her food.

The stork, which dwelleth on the fir treetop,
And trusteth that no power shall her dismay,
As kings on their high stations place their hope,
Nor wist that there be higher far than they:
The gay gier-eagle, beautiful to view,
Bearing within a savage heart untrue:

The ibis whom in Egypt Israel found,
Fell bird! That living serpents can digest;
The crested lapwing, wailing shrill around,
Solicitous, with no contentment blessed:
Last the foul bat, of bird, and beast first bred
Flitting, with little leathern sails dispread.

Thomas Warton the Elder (1688–1745)

PILGRIM SONG
(Deuteronomy 31.8)

On, O beloved children,
  The evening is at hand,
    And desolate and fearful
  The solitary land.
    Take heart! the rest eternal
Awaits our weary feet;
    From strength to strength press onwards,
  The end, how passing sweet!

Lo, we can tread rejoicing
  The narrow pilgrim road;
    We know the voice that calls us,
  We know our faithful God.
    Come, children, on to glory!
With every face set fast
    Towards the golden towers
Where we shall rest at last.

It was with voice of singing
  We left the land of night,
    To pass in glorious music
Far onward out of sight.
    O children, was it sorrow?
Though thousand worlds be lost,
    Our eyes have looked on Jesus,
And thus we count the cost.

The praising and the blaming,
  The storehouse and the mart,
    The mourning and the feasting,
  The glory and the art,
    The wisdom and the cunning,
Left far amid the gloom;
    We may not look behind us,
For we are going home.

Across the will of nature
  Leads on the path of God;
        Not where the flesh delighteth
  The feet of Jesus trod.
        O bliss to leave behind us
  The fetters of the slave,
        To leave ourselves behind us,
  The grave-clothes and the grave!

To speed, unburdened pilgrims,
  Glad, empty-handed, free;
        To cross the trackless deserts,
  And walk upon the sea;
        As strangers among strangers,
  No home beneath the sun;
        How soon the wanderings ended,
  The endless rest begun!

We pass the children playing,
  For evening shades fall fast;
        We pass the wayside flower –
  God's Paradise at last!
        If now the path be narrow
  And steep and rough and lone,
        If crags and tangles cross it,
  Praise God! we will go on.

We follow in his footsteps;
  What if our feet be torn?
        Where he has marked the pathway
  All hail the briar and thorn!
        Scarce seen, scarce heard, unreckoned,
  Despised, defamed, unknown,
        Or heard but by our singing,
  On, children! ever on!

  G. Tersteegen (1697–1769)

DEEP RIVER

Oh, don't you want to go to the gospel feast,
That promised land where all is peace,
Oh! don't you want to go to that promised land,
That land where all is peace?

Deep river,
My home is over Jordan,
Deep river, Lord,
I want to cross over into camp-ground.

Traditional Black American Spiritual

THE TEN COMMANDMENTS

One God in worship entertain,
Never take his name in vain;
Keep and guard your holy day;
To father and mother, honour pay;
Murder of men, put out of mind;
Never sin with womankind;
False oath, swear not;
False witness, bear not;
For wife of neighbour, see you never lust;
For goods of neighbour, have no greed unjust.

Good are these commandments ten:
Keep them strictly, all you men!
He who will not keep them well
Shall go down to deepest hell.
He who keeps them right
Shall go to heaven bright.

Anon. (Medieval)
Trans. Brian Stone

EV'RY TIME I FEEL THE SPIRIT

Ev'ry time I feel the Spirit
Movin' in my heart I will pray.

'Pon de mountain my Lord spoke,
Out his mouth came fire and smoke.

All a roun' me look so fine,
Ask my Lord if all was mine.

Jordan river chilly and cold,
Chills the body not the soul.

Ev'ry time I feel the Spirit
Movin' in my heart I will pray.

Traditional Black American Spiritual

THOU. . . SHALT TALK OF THEM WHEN THOU SITTEST IN THINE HOUSE
(Deuteronomy 6.7)

When quiet in my house I sit,
　Thy book be my companion still,
My joy Thy sayings to repeat,
　Talk o'er the records of Thy will,
And search the oracles divine,
Till every heartfelt word is mine.

Charles Wesley

GOD IN THE DESERT
(A meditation on Deuteronomy 32.9–14)

When in the wilderness my people faced
The agony of desert place and howling waste,
There I encircled you with love divine
And gently sought you, dearest child of mine.
I know the desert places you have known.
I came to seek you, loved one, as my own.
There I encircled you in wilderness
And sought to touch you with my love's caress.
There in that desert place so harsh and dry
I kept you even as *the apple of my eye*,
There like an eagle fluttering o'er its young
I flew beneath you while you fearful clung.
Spreading my pinions 'neath you, angel's wings,
I bore you up majestic, King of Kings.
I made you ride on high in realms of grace
Until at last you saw my Father's Face.
I fed you sweetest honey from the rock,
Curds from the herd and milk from my dear flock.
Yes, I the Shepherd God, the Great *I am*
Have journeyed with you through your desert, precious lamb.
There on dark Calvary I shed my blood
And gave my life for you, *the Lamb of God*.
For bread of life I gave you finest wheat
And for your thirst the gift of wine so sweet.
Red blood of grape, you drank, crushed on the precious vine.
O taste and see, this is my Love Divine.
I in the wilderness and the desert place,
Have come to you, my wounded child, with grace,
Grace now sufficient. I your Lord am nigh.
I smile on you in love, *the apple of my eye*.

David J. Payne (b. 1931)

THE
HISTORIES
(Joshua to Esther)

SAMSON AGONISTES
(An extract)

O dark, dark, dark, dark, dark, amid the blaze of noon,
Irrecoverably dark, total Eclipse
Without all hope of day!
O first created Beam, and thou great Word,
Let there be light, and light was over all;
Why am I thus bereaved thy prime decree?
The Sun to me is dark
And silent as the Moon,
When she deserts the night
Hid in her vacant interlunar cave.

John Milton (1608–74)

RAHAB

Her velvet sleeves lay motionless
And limp against the scarlet dress.
A half-said word hung still and thin
Between her frozen lips, and in
The distance she could hear the screams
Of men whose adolescent dreams
She metamorphosed into sin
Converting fantasy to skin.

No blinking now from bark-brown eyes,
But only blankness, while the skies
Above the city fill with smoke
From burning wives who used to stoke
The supper stove and wait for men
Who didn't come, allured again
By Rahab to the harlot's bed,
They'd sworn to see her dead.

But now, as always, there she stood,
As far from burning as she could,
And thought about a thousand nights
When she had watched the flames and flights
Of passion in her patron's play,
But kept her heart a mile away.

She watched until the sun went down
And all of Jericho's renown
Blew southward to the Salted Sea.
Then terrified and fearfully
She fell and spread her hands and face
Upon the ground, and to abase
Herself she scooped the dust and dirt
And threw it on her head and skirt
Until the last of strength was gone,
And then she wept until the dawn,
And choked out words repeatedly:
'Why was I spared? Why me? Why me?'

At dawn she heard a Jewish voice:
"Tis good to weep and not rejoice;
The sorrow first and then the song',
The words of Joshua were strong.
'Now rise and go down to the stream,
And make you clean – this is no dream!
The answer to your cry, "Why me?":
The God of Abraham is free.
His sun is rising in the east,
The priests have made for us a feast.
Go, make you clean and come with me;
There is another way to be.'
So Rahab made her face to shine
And took her place before the shrine.

John Piper (b. 1946)

SAMSON AND DELILAH
(From The History of Samson – Judges 16)

And afterward it came to pass he saw,
And lov'd a woman named Delilah,
Who in the vale of Sorek dwelt, to whom
There did the lords of the Philistines come,
And said, If thou wilt but entice him to reveal
Where lies his strength, and which way we may deal
With him, to bind him, to afflict him, we
Each one will give a great reward to thee.

And she to Samson said, I pray thee, tell
Wherein thy strength doth other men excel,
And how thou may'st be bound. And he replied,
If they with seven green withs that ne'er were dried,
Shall bind me hand and foot, I shall be then
As weak and impotent as other men.

Then the Philistine lords for her provide
The seven green withs which never had been dried,
And she therewith did bind him (now there were
Men lying in wait whom she had placed there),
Then she cried out, and said, Now Samson stand
Thy ground, for the Philistines are at hand.
And straight he brake the withs, and they became
Like to a thread of tow when touch'd with flame:
So was his strength not found out. Then said she,
Samson, behold, thou hast deceived me,
And told me lies: therefore no longer blind me,
But tell, I pray thee, wherewith I may bind thee.

Bind me with ropes that ne'er were us'd, said he;
Then weak as other men are, shall I be.
She therefore took new ropes, and bound him, and
Cried, Samson, the Philistines are at hand:
(And in the chamber there were men lay hid)
And from his arms he brake them like a thread.
Then said she, Thou hast mocked me hitherto,
And told me lies: now tell me what to do
To bind thee. He replied, Thou with the web
Must interweave the seven locks of my head.

Then she his locks did fasten with the pin,
And said, The Philistines are coming in,
Shift, Samson, for thyself; then he awoke,
And pin and web, and all away he took.
Then said she, How canst thou pretend to love me,
When thus thy doing towards me disprove thee?
For now, behold, thou hast deceived me thrice,
And hast not told me where thy great strength lies.

At length his soul being vex'd exceedingly,
By reason of her importunity:
He told the secrets of his heart, and said,
Never yet razor on my head was laid;
For I have been to God a Nazarite,
Even from the day that first I saw the light:
Wherefore like other men, if I am shaven,
I shall be weak, and of my strength bereaven.

And when she saw that he had told her all
The secrets of his heart, she sent to call
The lords of the Philistines. Come, said she,
This once, for now he hath made known to me
The very truth. Then they came up together,
And brought the money in their hands to give her.
Then down to sleep upon her knees she laid him,
And call'd a man, who of his locks betray'd him.
And to afflict him she began, and then
His strength became like that of other men.
Then said she, Samson, thy Philistine foes
Are just at hand: and he from sleep arose,
And as at other times went forth to shake him,
Not knowing that the Lord did now forsake him.

But the Philistines seized him, and brought
Him down to Gaza, having first put out
His eyes, and did with brazen fetters bind
And made him in the prison house to grind.
Howbeit the hair upon his head began,
After he had been shaved, to grow again.
John Bunyan

withs: bowstrings

SAMSON TO HIS DELILAH
(From Divine Epigrams)

Could not once blinding me, cruel, suffice?
When first I look'd on thee, I lost mine eyes.
Richard Crashaw (1612–49)

SAMSON AGONISTES

(An extract)

Blind among enemies, O worse then chains,
Dungeon, or beggery, or decrepit age!
Light the prime work of God to me is extinct,
And all her various objects of delight
Annulled, which might in part my grief have eased,
Inferior to the vilest now become
Of man or worm; the vilest here excel me,
They creep, yet see, I dark in light exposed
To daily fraud, contempt, abuse and wrong,
Within doors, or without, still as a fool,
In power of others, never in my own;
Scarce half I seem to live, dead more then half.
O dark, dark, dark, dark, dark, amid the blaze of noon,
Irrecoverably dark, total Eclipse
Without all hope of day!
O first created Beam, and thou great Word,
Let there be light, and light was over all;
Why am I thus bereaved thy prime decree?
The Sun to me is dark
And silent as the Moon,
When she deserts the night
Hid in her vacant interlunar cave.
Since light so necessary is to life,
And almost life itself, if it be true
That light is in the Soul,
She all in every part; why was the sight
To such a tender ball as the eye confined?
So obvious and so easy to be quenched,
And not as feeling through all parts diffused,
That she might look at will through every pore?
Then had I not been thus exiled from light;
As in the land of darkness yet in light,
To live a life half dead, a living death,
And buried; but O yet more miserable!
My self, my Sepulchre, a moving Grave,
Buried, yet not exempt
By privilege of death and burial

From worst of other evils, pains and wrongs,
But made hereby obnoxious more
To all the miseries of life,
Life in captivity
Among inhuman foes.
John Milton

THE BOOK OF RUTH
(An extract)

There was a man of kin to Naomi,
One that was of her husband's family,
His name was Boaz, and his wealth was great.
And Ruth, the Moabitess, did intreat
Her mother's leave, that she might go, and gather
Some ears of corn, where she should most find favour:
Go, daughter, go, said she. She went and came
Near to the reapers, to glean after them:
And lo, it was her hap to light among
The reapers, which to Boaz did belong.

Behold, now Boaz came from Bethlehem
Unto his reapers, and saluted them,
And they bless'd him again: and he enquired
Of him that was set over them he hired,
From whence the damsel was, and was informed
She was the Moabitess that returned
With Naomi: and she did ask, said he,
That here amongst the reapers she might be,
And that she might have liberty to glean
Among the sheaves. And she all day hath been,
Ev'n from the morning until now, with us,
That she hath stayed a little in the house.

Then Boaz said to Ruth, observe, my daughter,
That thou go not from hence, or follow after
The reapers of another field, but where
My maidens are, see that thou tarry there:
Observe what field they reap, and go thou there,
Have I not charged the young men to forbear
To touch thee? And when thou dost thirst, approach
And drink of what the youths have set abroach.

Then she fell on her face, and to the ground
She bow'd herself, and said, Why have I found
Such favour in thine eyes; that thou, to me
Who am a stranger, should so courteous be?
And Boaz said, it hath been fully shewn
To me, what to thy mother-in-law thou'st done,
Since of thine husband thou hast been bereft:
How thou thy father and thy mother left,
And thine own native land; to come unto
A land which thou before didst never know:
The Lord, the God of Israel, the defence
Whom now thou'st chosen, be thy recompence.

Then said she, let me in thy sight, my lord,
Find favour in that thou dost thus afford
Me comfort, and since thou so kind to me
Dost speak, though I thereof unworthy be.
And Boaz said, at meal time come thou near,
Eat of the bread, and dip i' the vinegar.
And by the reapers she sat down to meat,
He gave her parched corn, and she did eat,
And was sufficed; and left, and rose to glean:
And Boaz gave command to the young men,
Let her come in among the sheaves, said he,
To glean, and let her not reproached be.
Let fall some handfuls also purposely,
And let her take them without injury.

So she till even gleaned, and then beat out
Her barley, being an ephah or thereabout.
She took it up, and to the city went,
And to her mother-in-law did it present:
And what she had reserved to her she gave,

When she had took what she designed to have.

Then unto her, her mother-in-law did say,
In what field hast thou been to glean to-day?
And where hast thou been working? Blest be he,
That thus hath taken cognizance of thee.
She told with whom, and furthermore did say,
The man's name's Boaz, where I wrought to-day.
And Naomi replied, may he be blest,
Even of the Lord, whose kindness manifest
Unto the living and the dead hath been:
The man's our kinsman, yea, the next of kin.
And Ruth, the Moabitess, said, he gave
Me likewise a commandment not to leave,
Or to depart from following his young men,
Until they had brought all his harvest in.

And Naomi said unto Ruth, my daughter,
'Tis good that thou observe to follow after
His maidens, that they meet thee not elsewhere.
So she to Boaz's maidens still kept near,
Till barley and wheat harvest both, she saw
Were done, and she dwelt with her mother-in-law.
John Bunyan

SAUL

(An extract)

I
Said Abner, 'At last thou art come! Ere I tell, ere thou speak,
Kiss my cheek, wish me well!' Then I wished it, and did kiss his
    cheek.
And he: 'Since the King, O my friend, for thy countenance sent,
Neither drunken nor eaten have we; nor until from his tent
Thou return with the joyful assurance the King liveth yet,
Shall our lip with the honey be bright, with the water be wet.
For out of the black mid-tent's silence, a space of three days,
Not a sound hath escaped to thy servants, of prayer nor of praise,
To betoken that Saul and the Spirit have ended their strife,
And that, faint in his triumph, the monarch sinks back upon life.

II

'Yet now my heart leaps, O beloved! God's child with His dew
On thy gracious gold hair, and those lilies still living and blue
Just broken to twine round thy harp-strings, as if no wild heat
Were now raging to torture the desert!'

III

Then I, as was meet,
Knelt down to the God of my fathers, and rose on my feet,
And ran o'er the sand burnt to powder. The tent was unlooped;
I pulled up the spear that obstructed, and under I stooped;
Hands and knees on the slippery grass-patch, all withered and gone,
That extends to the second enclosure, I groped my way on
Till I felt where the fold-skirts fly open. Then once more I prayed,
And opened the fold-skirts and entered, and was not afraid
But spoke, 'Here is David, thy servant!' And no voice replied.
At the first I saw naught but the blackness: but soon I descried
A something more black than the blackness – the vast, the upright
Main prop which sustains the pavilion: and slow into sight
Grew a figure against it, gigantic and blackest of all.
Then a sunbeam, that burst through the tent-roof, showed Saul.

IV

He stood as erect as that tent-prop, both arms stretched out wide
On the great cross-support in the centre, that goes to each side;
He relaxed not a muscle, but hung there as, caught in his pangs
And waiting his change, the king-serpent all heavily hangs,
Far away from his kind, in the pine, till deliverance come
With the spring-time, – so agonized Saul, drear and stark, blind and
    dumb.

V

Then I tuned my harp, – took off the lilies we twine round its chords
Lest they snap 'neath the stress of the noontide – those sunbeams like
    swords!
And I first played the tune all our sheep know, as, one after one,
So docile they come to the pen-door till folding be done.
They are white and untorn by the bushes, for lo, they have fed
Where the long grasses stifle the water within the stream's bed;
And now one after one seeks its lodging, as star follows star
Into eve and the blue far above us, – so blue and so far!

VI

Then the tune for which quails on the corn-land will each leave his
    mate
To fly after the player; then, what makes the crickets elate
Till for boldness they fight one another; and then, what has weight
To set the quick jerboa a-musing outside his sand house –
There are none such as he for a wonder, half bird and half mouse!
God made all the creatures and gave them our love and our fear,
To give sign, we and they are his children, one family here.

VII

Then I played the help-tune of our reapers, their wine-song, when
    hand
Grasps at hand, eye lights eye in good friendship, and great hearts
    expand
And grow one in the sense of this world's life. – And then, the last
    song
When the dead man is praised on his journey – 'Bear, bear him
    along,
With his few faults shut up like dead flowerets! Are balm seeds not
    here
To console us? The land has none left such as he on the bier.
Oh, would we might keep thee, my brother!' – And then, the glad
    chaunt
Of the marriage, – first go the young maidens, next, she whom we
    vaunt
As the beauty, the pride of our dwelling. – And then, the great march
Wherein man runs to man to assist him and buttress an arch
Nought can break; who shall harm them, our friends? Then, the
    chorus intoned
As the Levites go up to the altar in glory enthroned.
But I stopped here: for here in the darkness Saul groaned.

VIII

And I paused, held my breath in such silence, and listened apart;
And the tent shook, for mighty Saul shuddered: and sparkles 'gan dart
From the jewels that woke in his turban, at once, with a start,
All its lordly male-sapphires, and rubies courageous at heart.
So the head: but the body still moved not, still hung there erect.
And I bent once again to my playing, pursued it unchecked,
As I sang, –

IX

'Oh, our manhood's prime vigour! No spirit feels waste,
Not a muscle is stopped in its playing nor sinew unbraced.
Oh, the wild joys of living! the leaping from rock up to rock,
The strong rending of boughs from the fir-tree, the cool silver shock
Of the plunge in a pool's living water, the hunt of the bear,
And the sultriness showing the lion is couched in his lair.
And the meal, the rich dates yellowed over with gold dust divine,
And the locust-flesh steeped in the pitcher, the full draught of wine,
And the sleep in the dried river-channel where bulrushes tell
That the water was wont to go warbling so softly and well.
How good is man's life, the mere living! how fit to employ
All the heart and the soul and the senses forever in joy!
Hast thou loved the white locks of thy father, whose sword thou didst
    guard
When he trusted thee forth with the armies, for glorious reward?
Didst thou see the thin hands of thy mother, held up as men sung
The low song of the nearly-departed, and hear her faint tongue
Joining in while it could to the witness, "Let one more attest,
I have lived, seen God's hand, thro' a life-time, and all was for best?"
Then they sung through their tears in strong triumph, not much, but
    the rest.
And thy brothers, the help and the contest, the working whence grew
Such result as, from seething grape-bundles, the spirit strained true:
And the friends of thy boyhood – that boyhood of wonder and hope,
Present promise and wealth of the future beyond the eye's scope, –
Till lo, thou art grown to a monarch; a people is thine;
And all gifts, which the world offers singly, on one head combine!
On one head, all the beauty and strength, love and rage (like the throe
That, a-work in the rock, helps its labour and lets the gold go)
High ambition and deeds which surpass it, fame crowning them, – all
Brought to blaze on the head of one creature – King Saul!'
Robert Browning (1812–89)

A SONG TO DAVID
(An extract)

Sweet is the dew that falls betimes,
And drops upon the leafy limes;
Sweet Hermon's fragrant air:
Sweet is the lily's silver bell,
And sweet the wakeful tapers smell
That watch for early pray'r.

Sweet the young nurse with love intense,
Which smiles o'er sleeping innocence;
Sweet when the lost arrive:
Sweet the musician's ardour beats,
While his vague mind's in quest of sweets,
The choicest flow'rs to hive.

Sweeter in all the strains of love,
The language of thy turtle dove,
Pair'd to thy swelling chord;
Sweeter with ev'ry grace endu'd,
The glory of thy gratitude,
Respir'd unto the Lord.

Strong is the horse upon his speed;
Strong in pursuit the rapid glede,
Which makes at once his game:
Strong the tall ostrich on the ground;
Strong thro' the turbulent profound
Shoots xiphias to his aim.

Strong is the lion – like a coal
His eye-ball – like a bastion's mole
His chest against the foes:
Strong, the gier-eagle on his sail,
Strong against tide, th' enormous whale
Emerges as he goes.

But stronger still, in earth and air,
And in the sea, the man of pray'r;
And far beneath the tide;
And in the seat to faith assign'd,
Where ask is have, where seek is find,
Where knock is open wide.

Beauteous the fleet before the gale;
Beauteous the multitudes in mail,
Rank'd arms and crested heads:
Beauteous the garden's umbrage mild,
Walk, water, meditated wild,
And all the bloomy beds.

Beauteous the moon full on the lawn;
And beauteous, when the veil's withdrawn,
The virgin to her spouse:
Beauteous the temple deck'd and fill'd,
When to the heav'n of heav'ns they build
Their heart-directed vows.

Beauteous, yea beauteous more than these,
The shepherd king upon his knees,
For his momentous trust;
With wish of infinite conceit,
For man, beast, mute, the small and great,
And prostrate dust to dust.

Precious the bounteous widow's mite;
And precious, for extreme delight,
The largess from the churl:
Precious the ruby's blushing blaze,
And alba's blest imperial rays,
And pure cerulean pearl.

Precious the penitential tear;
And precious is the sigh sincere,
Acceptable to God:
And precious are the winning flow'rs,
In gladsome Israel's feast of bow'rs,
Bound on the hallow'd sod.

More precious that diviner part
Of David, ev'n the Lord's own heart,
Great, beautiful, and new:
In all things where it was intent,
In all extremes, in each event,
Proof – answ'ring true to true.

Glorious the sun in mid career;
Glorious th' assembled fires appear;
Glorious the comet's train:
Glorious the trumpet and alarm;
Glorious th' almighty stretch'd-out arm;
Glorious th' enraptur'd main:

Glorious the northern lights a-stream;
Glorious the song, when God's the theme;
Glorious the thunder's roar:
Glorious hosanna from the den;
Glorious the catholic amen;
Glorious the martyr's gore:

Glorious – more glorious is the crown
Of Him that brought salvation down
By meekness, call'd thy Son;
Thou that stupendous truth believ'd,
And now the matchless deed's achiev'd,
Determin'd, dar'd, and done.

Christopher Smart (1722–71)

PUT ON YOUR PURPLE, ESTHER!

Put on your purple, Esther, Esther;
Esther, put on your crown of gold,
And go and wait
By the King's own gate –
For your people will perish, Esther, Esther,
Unless your heart is bold!

She put on her purple and crown, did Esther;
Esther she did as she was told.
She broke the Law,
But the King, who saw,
Said, 'She is beautiful, Esther, Esther!'
And held out his rod of gold.

Eleanor Farjeon

THE
WISDOM BOOKS
(Job to Song of Songs)

PSALM 52
(An extract)

I as an olive tree
Still green shall flourish:
God's house the soil shall be
My roots to nourish.

Mary Herbert, Countess of Pembroke (1561–1621)

OH THAT I KNEW WHERE
I MIGHT FIND HIM!
(Job 23.3)

Where but on yonder tree?
Or if too rich thou art,
   Sink into poverty,
And find him in thine heart.
Charles Wesley

'WHOM I SHALL SEE FOR MYSELF'
(Job 19.27)

I know that my Redeemer lives,
He lives, and on the earth shall stand;
And though to worms my flesh he gives,
My dust lies numbered in his hand.

In this re-animated clay
I surely shall behold him near;
Shall see him in the latter day
In all his majesty appear.

I feel what then shall raise me up,
The eternal Spirit lives in me;
This is my confidence of hope,
That God I face to face shall see.

Mine own and not another's eyes
The King shall in his beauty view;
I shall from him receive the prize,
The starry crown to victors due.
Charles Wesley

'WHY DOST THOU SHADE THY LOVELY FACE?'

('Wherefore hidest thou thy Face, and holdest me
for thy enemy' – Job 13.24)

Why dost thou shade thy lovely face? Oh, why
Does that eclipsing hand so long deny
The sunshine of thy soul-enliv'ning eye?

Without that light, what light remains in me?
Thou art my life, my way, my light; in thee
I live, I move, and by thy beams I see.

Thou art my life; if thou but turn away
My life's a thousand deaths: thou art my way;
Without thee, Lord, I travel not, but stray.

My light thou art; without thy glorious sight
Mine eyes are darken'd with perpetual night.
My God, thou art my way, my life, my light.

Thou art my way; I wander if thou fly:
Thou art my light; if hid, how blind am I!
Thou art my life; if thou withdraw, I die.

Mine eyes are blind and dark, I cannot see;
To whom or whither should my darkness flee,
But to the light? and who's that light but thee?

My path is lost, my wand'ring steps do stray;
I cannot safely go, nor safely stay;
Whom should I seek but thee, my path, my way?

Oh, I am dead: to whom shall I, poor I,
Repair? to whom shall my sad ashes fly,
But life? and where is life but in thine eye?

And yet thou turn'st away thy face, and fly'st me;
And yet I sue for grace, and thou deny'st me;
Speak, art thou angry, Lord, or only try'st me?

Unscreen those heavenly lamps, or tell me why
Thou shad'st thy face; perhaps thou think'st no eye
Can view those flames, and not drop down and die.

If that be all, shine forth, and draw thee nigher;
Let me behold and die, for my desire
Is phoenix-like to perish in that fire.

Death-conquer'd Laz'rus was redeem'd by thee;
If I am dead, Lord, set death's prisoner free;
Am I more spent, or stink I worse than he?

If my puff'd life be out, give leave to tine
My shameless snuff at that bright lamp of thine;
Oh, what's thy light the less for lighting mine?

If I have lost my path, great Shepherd, say,
Shall I still wander in a doubtful way?
Lord, shall a lamb of Israel's sheep-fold stray?

Thou art the pilgrim's path, the blind man's eye,
The dead man's life; on thee my hopes rely;
If thou remove, I err, I grope, I die.

Disclose thy sunbeams; close thy wings, and stay;
See, see how I am blind, and dead, and stray,
O thou, that art my light, my life, my way.

Francis Quarles (1592–1644)

tine: kindle

THE COMPLAINT OF NATURE
(Job 24.1–15)

Few are thy days and full of woe,
    O man, of woman born!
Thy doom is written, 'Dust thou art,
    And shalt to dust return.'

Behold the emblem of thy state
    In flowers that bloom and die,
Or in the shadow's fleeting form,
    That mocks the gazer's eye.

Guilty and frail, how shalt thou stand
    Before thy sov'reign Lord?
Can troubled and polluted springs
    A hallow'd stream afford?

Determin'd are the days that fly
    Successive o'er thy head;
The number'd hour is on the wing
    That lays thee with the dead.

Great God! Afflict not in thy wrath
    The short allotted span
That bounds the few and weary days
    Of pilgrimage to man.

All nature dies, and lives again
    The flow'r that paints the field
The trees that crown the mountain's brow
    And boughs and blossoms yield.

Resign the honours of their form
    At Winter's stormy blast
And leave the naked leafless plain
    A desolated waste.

Yet soon reviving plants and flow'rs
    Anew shall deck the plain;
The woods shall hear the voice of Spring,
    And flourish green again.

But man departs this earthly scene,
    Ah! Never to return:
Shall any foll'wing Spring revive
    The ashes of the urn?

The mighty flood that rolls along
    Its torrents to the main
Can ne'er recall its waters lost
    From that abyss again.

So days and years and ages past
    Descending down to night
Can henceforth never more return
    Back to the gates of light;

And man when laid in lonesome grave
    Shall sleep in Death's dark gloom,
Until th' eternal morning wake
    The slumbers of the tomb.

O may the grave become to me
    The bed of peaceful rest,
Whence I shall gladly rise at length,
    And mingle with the blest!

Cheer'd by this hope, with patient mind,
    I'll wait Heav'ns high decree
Till the appointed period come
    When death shall set me free.

Michael Bruce (1746–67)

THE LORD GOD OMNIPOTENT
(Job 36.6–14)

Who can resist th' Almighty arm
    That made the starry sky?
Or who elude the certain glance
    Of God's all-seeing eye?

From him no cov'ring vails our crimes;
    Hell opens to his sight;
And all Destruction's secret snares
    Lie full disclos'd in light.

Firm on the boundless void of space
    He pois'd the steady pole,
And in the circle of his clouds
    Bade secret waters roll.

While nature's universal frame
   Its Maker's powers reveals,
His throne, remote from mortal eyes,
   And awful cloud conceals.

From whence the rising day ascends,
   To where it sets in night,
He compasses the floods with bounds,
   And checks their threat'ning might.

The pillars that support the sky
   Tremble at his rebuke;
Through all its caverns quakes the earth
   As though its centre shook.

He brings the waters from their beds,
   Although no tempest blows,
And smites the kingdom of the proud
   Without the hand of foes.

With bright inhabitants above
   He fills the heav'nly land,
And all the crooked serpent's breed
   Dismay'd before him stand.

Few of his works can we survey;
   These few our skill transcend:
But the full thunder of his pow'r
   What heart can comprehend?
Michael Bruce

PS. 19

Clean is the word with *fear*.
Fear is to love high
and know longing for clear
sunlight, to the last ribcorner
and capillary – and wonder
if, so known, a sighing–

over-the-marshlands me
might all evaporate, wisp away.
Yet to love high
is with this very fear
to shrink *and* seek to be made plain,
openly to own
both the mists smoking from pure
stone-cold lake-still sun-sweetened places
and the dank mist that rises
from the long-unsunned, sour
pools, hid even from the storm's sluices.

Enduring is the word with *clean*.
The fear once won
of sunward love, it proves – not boulderstone,
baldness, slowly in fire consuming – but green
with life, moss, cup-rock-water, cliff riven
for a springing pine;
and thus, trusted to fire, drawn
towards an enduring sun.
Margaret Avison (b. 1918)

O GOD WHO SHAPED THE
STARRY SKIES
(Based on Psalm 19.7–11)

O God who shaped the starry skies
and made the sun in splendour rise,
    whose love our life imparts,
still may that same creative word
which formless void and darkness heard
    be known within our hearts.

Teach us to see, as Moses saw,
your will revealed in perfect law,
    a covenant divine;
a word to make the simple wise,
a light of truth before our eyes,
    and on our souls to shine.

Move every heart in holy fear
the judgments of the Lord to hear,
    your word about our way;
and in that law let all rejoice
to find a loving Father's voice
    and his command obey.

So may we share for evermore
the sweetness of that golden store,
    and taste its rich reward;
and make the Scriptures our delight
and walk as pleasing in your sight,
    our great redeeming Lord.
    Timothy Dudley-Smith

PSALM 19

I
All glory to God deep heaven declares;
From skies his handicraft cries, and is taught.
His words the east-west flowing days report,
And their nights uncurtain knowledge. Earth shares
The auditorium, we all have chairs
In which to listen – all our senses caught,
Unless we are deceived. Those fooled distort
What they see, null their world, relish nightmares

While God sets star-skied, a tent for the sun,
The anticipant sun – like groom before
Bride, like athlete eager to start her run.
The sun skirts our wide astral sea from shore
To shore; ends where firm-circle was begun.
None escape its firm heat, its oak life door.

II
God's law is faultless, unmaking our bent;
God's oak-firm witness enwises dim mind;
His statutes make sense, make joy to heart bind.
God-awe, clean, is ever-circle of tent:

From God's pure commandment sunlight is sent:
His straight judgments are sun-heat firm, but kind.

These ghosts, words of God weigh more than refined,
Fine-wrought gold and artworks. Far more is meant
By them than quiet after noise, green sights
Fresh after grey city work. They also
Warn God's servant: great wages, great delights
Are ours in keeping them! Yet who can know
Straightness beside their straightness? Hear my night's
Words, Lord! Free me from the Fall's great woe!
Colin Duriez

THOU MY SHIELD AND THOU MY LIGHT
(Psalm 27)

Thou my shield and Thou my light,
I will not fear in darkest fight.
In war and peace my one delight
That I can live to praise Thy name.

And tho' hosts of hell be sent
In spite of all their cruel intent
In this will I be confident
that I can live to praise Thy name.

One thing, Lord, I've longed of Thee;
Thine own to be, Thy face to see;
Now make Thy temple home to me,
And I will live to praise Thy name.

Tho' by death all friends forsake,
Yet in His arms the Lord will take,
Till from the dust His call shall wake,
Then will I live to praise His name.
Linette Martin (1937–98)

PSALM 52
(An extract)

I as an olive tree
   Still green shall flourish:
God's house the soil shall be
   My roots to nourish.

My trust on his true love
   Truly attending,
Shall never thence remove,
   Never see ending.

Thee will I honour still,
   Lord, for this justice;
There fix my hopes I will
   Where thy saints' trust is.

Thy saints trust in thy name,
   Therein they joy them:
Protected by the same,
   Naught can annoy them.

Mary Herbert, Countess of Pembroke

MAN FRAIL AND GOD ETERNAL
(Psalm 90.1–5)

Our God, our help in ages past,
Our hope for years to come,
Our shelter from the stormy blast,
And our eternal home.
Under the shadow of thy throne
Thy Saints have dwelt secure;
Sufficient is thine arm alone,
And our defence is sure.
Before the hills in order stood,
Or earth receiv'd her frame,
From everlasting thou art God,
To endless years the same.

Thy word commands our flesh to dust,
'Return, ye sons of men':
All nations rose from earth at first,
And turn to earth again.
A thousand ages in thy sight
Are like an ev'ning gone;
Short as the watch that ends the night,
Before the rising sun.
The busy tribes of flesh and blood,
With all their lives and cares,
Are carry'd downwards by the flood,
And lost in following years.
Time, like an ever-rolling stream,
Bears all his sons away;
They fly, forgotten, as a dream
Dies at the op'ning day.
Like flow'ry fields the nations stand,
Pleas'd with the morning light:
The flow'rs beneath the mower's hand
Lie with'ring ere 'tis night.
Our God, our help in ages past,
Our hope for years to come,
Be thou our guard while troubles last,
And our eternal home.
Isaac Watts (1674–1748)

PSALM 100

All people that on earth do dwell,
    Sing to the Lord, with cheerful voice
Him serve with fear, his praise forth tell,
    Come ye before him and rejoice.

The Lord ye know is God in deed,
    With out our aide, he did us make:
We are his flock, he doth us feed,
    And for his Sheep, he doth us take.

Oh enter then his gates with praise
    Approach with joy, his courts unto:
Praise, laude, and bless his name always,
    For it is seemly so to doe.

For why? the Lord our God is good,
    His mercy is for ever sure:
His truth at all times firmly stood
    And shall from age to age endure.
William Kethe (d. 1608?)

LORD, HEAR MY PRAYER
(A Paraphrase of Psalm 102)

Lord, hear my prayer when trouble glooms,
Let sorrow find a way,
And when the day of trouble comes,
Turn not thy face away:
My bones like hearthstones burn away,
My life like vapoury smoke decays.

My heart is smitten like the grass,
That withered lies and dead,
And I, so lost to what I was,
Forget to eat my bread.
My voice is groaning all the day,
My bones prick through this skin of clay.

The wilderness's pelican,
The desert's lonely owl –
I am their like, a desert man
In ways as lone and foul.
As sparrow on the cottage top
I wait till I with fainting drop.

I hear my enemies reproach,
All silently I mourn;
They on my private peace encroach,
Against me they are sworn.

Ashes as bread my trouble shares,
And mix my food with weeping cares.

Yet not for them is sorrow's toil,
I fear no mortal frowns –
But thou hast held me up awhile
And thou hast cast me down.
My days like shadows waste from view,
I mourn like withered grass in dew.

But thou, Lord, shalt endure for ever,
All generations through;
Thou shalt to Zion be the giver
Of joy and mercy too.
Her very stones are in thy trust,
Thy servants reverence her dust.

Heathens shall hear and fear thy name,
All kings of earth thy glory know
When thou shalt build up Zion's fame
And live in glory there below
He'll not despise their prayers, though mute,
But still regard the destitute.

John Clare (1793–1864)

FROM PSALM 107

Let men therefore before the Lord
    Confess his kindness then;
And shew the wonders that he doth
    Before the sons of men
And let them offer sacrifice
    With thanks, and also fear;
And speak of all his wondrous works
    With glad and joyful cheer.

Such as in ships and brittle barks
    Into the seas descend,
Their merchandise through fearful floods
    To compass and to end;

Those men are forcèd to behold
   The Lord's works what they be,
And in the dangerous deep, the same
   Most marvellous they see.

For at his word the stormy wind
   Ariseth in a rage,
And stirreth up the surges so
   As naught can them assuage.
Then are they lifted up so high
   The clouds they seem to gain,
And plunging down the depth until
   Their souls consume with pain.

And like a drunkard, to and fro
   Now here now there they reel,
As men with fear of wit bereft
   Or had of sense no feel.
Then did they cry in their distress
   Unto the Lord for aid;
Who did remove their troublous state,
   According as they pray'd.

For with his word the Lord doth make
   The sturdy storms to cease;
So that the great waves from their rage
   Are brought to rest and peace.
Then are men glad when rest is come
   Which they so much did crave;
And are by him in haven brought,
   Which they so fain would have.

William Kethe

PSALM 117

Praise him that ay
Remains the same:
All tongues display
Iehovas fame.
Sing all that share
This earthy ball:

His mercies are
Expos'd to all:
Like as the word
Once he doth give,
Rold in record,
Doth tyme outlive.

Mary Herbert,
Countess of Pembroke

(This poem forms an acrostic, with the initial letters of the lines
reading, 'Prais' the Lord'.)

I LIFT MY EYES
(Based on Psalm 121)

I lift my eyes
to the quiet hills
in the press of a busy day;
   as green hills stand
   in a dusty land
as God is my strength and stay.

I lift my eyes
to the quiet hills
to a calm that is mine to share;
   secure and still
   in the Father's will
and kept by the Father's care.

I lift my eyes
to the quiet hills
with a prayer as I turn to sleep;
   by day, by night,
   through the dark and light
my shepherd will guard his sheep.

I lift my eyes
to the quiet hills
and my heart to the Father's throne;
   in all my ways
     to the end of days
the Lord will preserve his own.

Timothy Dudley-Smith

PSALM 125

As Sion standeth very firmly steadfast,
Never once shaking: so, on high, Jehovah
Who his hope buildeth, very firmly steadfast
     Ever abideth.

As Salem braveth with her hilly bulwarks
Roundly enforted: so the great Jehovah
Closeth his servants, as a hilly bulwark
     Ever abiding;

Though Tyrant's hard yoke with a heavy pressure
Wring the just shoulders: but a while it holdeth
Lest the best minded by too hard abusing
     Bend to abuses.

As to the well-workers, so the right believers;
Lord favour further; but a vain deceiver,
Whose wryèd footing not aright directed
     Wand'reth in error,

Lord him, abjected, set among the number
Whose doings lawless, study bent to mischief
Mischief expecteth: but upon thy chosen
     Peace be for ever.

Mary Herbert, Countess of Pembroke

PSALM 126

When God restored our captive state,
Joy was our song, and grace our theme;
The grace, beyond our hope so great,
That joy appeared a painted dream.

The scoffer owns thy hand, and pays
Unwilling honours to thy name;
While we, with pleasure, shout thy praise –
With cheerful notes thy love proclaim.

When we review our dismal fears,
'Twas hard to think they'd vanish so:
With God we left our flowing tears;
He makes our joys like rivers flow.

The man that in his furrowed field
His scattered seed with sadness leaves
Will shout to see the harvest yield
A welcome load of joyful sheaves.

Isaac Watts

PSALM 136

Let us with a gladsome mind
Praise the Lord, for he is kind,
   For his mercies aye endure,
   Ever faithful, ever sure.

Let us blaze his Name abroad,
For of gods he is the God;
   For his, etc.

Oh let us his praises tell,
Who doth the wrathful tyrants quell.
   For his, etc.

Who with his miracles doth make
Amazèd Heav'n and Earth to shake.
   For his, etc.

Who by his wisdom did create
The painted Heav'ns so full of state.
  For his, etc.

Who did the solid Earth ordain
To rise above the wat'ry plain.
  For his, etc.

Who by his all-Commanding might
Did fill the new-made world with light.
  For his, etc.

And caused the Golden-tressèd Sun
All the day long his course to run.
  For his, etc.

The horned Moon to Shine by night,
Amongst her spangled sisters bright.
  For his, etc.

He with his thunder-clasping hand
Smote the first-born of *Egypt* Land.
  For his, etc.

And in despite of *Pharaoh* fell,
He brought from thence his *Israël*
  For his, etc.

The ruddy waves he cleft in *twain*
Of the *Erythraean* main.
  For his, etc.

The floods stood still like Walls of Glass,
While the Hebrew Bands did pass.
  For his, etc.

But full soon they did devour
The Tawny King with all his power.
  For his, etc.

His chosen people he did bless
In the wasteful Wilderness.
  For his, etc.

In bloody battle he brought down
Kings of prowess and renown.
　　For his, etc.

He foiled bold *Seon* and his host,
That ruled the *Amorrean* coast.
　　For his, etc.

And large-limbed *Og* he did subdue,
With all his over-hardy crew.
　　For his, etc.

And to his Servant *Israël*
He gave their Land therein to dwell.
　　For his, etc.

He hath with a piteous eye
Beheld us in our misery.
　　For his, etc.

And freed us from the slavery
Of the invading enemy.
　　For his, etc.

All living creatures he doth feed,
And with full hand supplies their need.
　　For his, etc.

Let us therefore warble forth
His mighty Majesty and worth.
　　For his, etc.

That his mansion hath on high
Above the reach of mortal eye.
　　For his mercies aye endure,
　　Ever faithful, ever sure.

John Milton

PSALM 147

Sing to the Lord, for what can better be
    Than of our God that we the honour sing?
With seemly pleasure what can more agree
    Than praiseful voice and touch of tunèd string?
    For lo, the Lord again to form doth bring
        Jerusalem's long ruinated walls;
And Jacob's house, which all the earth did see
        Dispersèd erst, to union now recalls;
And now by him their broken hearts made sound,
    And now by him their bleeding wounds are bound.

For what could not, who can the number tell
    Of stars, the torches of his heav'nly hall;
And tell so readily, he knoweth well
    How ev'ry star by proper name to call?
    What great to him, whose greatness doth not fall
        Within precincts? Whose power no limits stay?
Whose knowledges all number so excel
        Not numb'ring number can their number lay?
Easy to him, to lift the lowly just;
    Easy, to down proud wicked to the dust.

O then Jehovah's causeful honour sing,
    His, whom our God we by his goodness find!
O make harmonious mix of voice and string
    To him by whom the skies with clouds are lin'd;
    By whom the rain, from clouds to drop assign'd,
        Supples the clods of summer-scorchèd fields,
Fresheth the mountains with such needful spring,
        Fuel of life to mountain cattle yields,
From whom young ravens careless old forsake,
    Croaking to him of alms, their diet take.

The stately shape, the force of bravest steed,
    Is far too weak to work in him delight;
No more to him can any pleasure breed
    In flying footman, foot of nimblest flight.
    Nay, which is more, his fearers in his sight
        Can well of nothing but his bounty brave;

Which, never failing, never lets them need
      Who fix'd their hopes upon his mercies have.
O then, Jerusalem, Jehovah praise,
      With honour due thy God, O Sion, raise.

His strength it is thy gates doth surely bar;
      His grace in thee thy children multiples;
By him thy borders lie secure from wars,
      And finest flour thy hunger satisfies.
      Nor means he needs; for fast his pleasure flies
          Borne by his word, when aught him list to bid.
Snow's woolly locks by him wide scatter'd are,
      And hoary plains with frost, as ashes, hid;
Gross icy gobbets from his hand he flings,
      And blows a cold too strong for strongest things.

He bids again, and ice in water flows,
      As water erst in ice congealèd lay;
Abroad the southern wind, his melter, goes;
      The streams relenting take their wonted way.
      O much is this, but more I come to say:
          The words of life he hath to Jacob told;
Taught Israel, who by his teaching knows
      What laws in life, what rule he wills to hold.
No nation else hath found him half so kind
      For to his light, what other is not blind?

Mary Herbert, Countess of Pembroke

PSALM 148

Praise the Lord! Ye heavens, adore him;
      Praise him, angels in the height;
Sun and moon, rejoice before him;
      Praise him, all ye stars and light.
Praise the Lord, for he hath spoken;
      Worlds his mighty voice obeyed;
Laws, which never shall be broken,
      For their guidance hath he made.

Praise the Lord, for he is glorious;
    Never shall his promise fail;
God hath made his saints victorious;
    Sin and death shall not prevail.
Praise the God of our salvation;
    Hosts on high, his power proclaim;
Heaven and earth and all creation,
    Laud and magnify his name.
Anon.

TO HIM WITH TRUMPETS
(See Psalm 150)

To him with trumpets and with flutes,
With comets, clarions, and with lutes,
With harps, with organs, and with shawms,
With holy anthems and with psalms,
With voice of angels and of men,
Sing Aleluyia: amen, amen.
Sir John Davies (1569–1626)

shawm: double-reed oboe-like instrument introduced to Europe
    during the Crusades

THE CALL OF WISDOM
(Proverbs 1.20–31)

In streets, and op'nings of the gates
    Where pours the busy crowd
Thus Heav'nly Wisdom lifts her voice,
    And cries to men aloud:

How long ye scorners of the truth,
    Scornful will ye remain?
How long shall fools their folly love,
    And hear my words in vain?

O turn, at last, at my reproof!
    And, in that happy hour,
His bless'd effusions on your heart
    My Spirit down shall pour.

But since so long, with earnest voice
    To you in vain I call,
Since all my counsels and reproofs
    Ineffectual fall:

The time will come, when humbled low
    In Sorrow's evil day,
Your voice by anguish shall be taught,
    But taught too late, to pray.

When, like the whirlwind, o'er the deep
    Comes Desolation's blast,
Pray'rs then extorted shall be vain,
    The hour of mercy past.

The choice you made has fix'd your doom;
    For this is Heav'n's decree,
That with the fruits of what he sow'd
    The sinner fill'd shall be.
Michael Bruce

HEARING WISDOM'S VOICE
(Proverbs 3.13–17)

O happy is the man who hears
    Instruction's warning voice;
And who celestial Wisdom makes
    His early, only choice.

For she has treasures greater far
    Than east or west unfold;
And her rewards more precious are
    Than all their stores of gold.

In her right hand she holds to view
  A length of happy days;
Riches, with splendid honours join'd,
  Are what her left displays.

She guides the young with innocence,
  In pleasure's paths to tread,
A crown of glory she bestows
  Upon the hoary head.

According to her labours rise,
  So her rewards increase;
Her ways are ways of pleasantness,
  And all her paths are peace.
Michael Bruce

FOR EVERYTHING THERE IS A SEASON
(Ecclesiastes 3)

The time to weep is the heart's winter.
    Grief is the grip of ice and silence,
snow and vast grey skies. Bending under
    tree-caught snow, nerves hold the sad immense.

The time to laugh is when new is sprung
    suddenly. Renewal – new love, new
light, new green, new morning, blossom hung
    delight – makes the Spring of the heart due.

There is a time for living. Into
    a wide green under a thoughtful sun
we move and struggle. What is the true
    must reach here, must judge what we have done.

There is also a time for dying.
    The green leaves become brown, the grass fades,
the unplucked fruit drops and rots. Sighing
    tree-sung rain makes cold, decaying shades.

Colin Duriez

ALL IS VANITY, SAITH THE PREACHER
(See Ecclesiastes 12.8)

Fame, wisdom, love, and power were mine,
    And health and youth possessed me;
My goblets blushed from every vine,
    And lovely forms caressed me;
I sunned my heart in beauty's eyes,
    And felt my soul grow tender
All earth can give, or mortal prize,
    Was mine of regal splendour.

I strive to number o'er what days
    Remembrance can discover,
Which all that life or earth displays
    Would lure me to live over.
There rose no day, there rolled no hour
    Of pleasure unembittered;
And not a trapping decked my power
    That galled not while it glittered.

The serpent of the field, by art
    And spells, is won from harming
But that which coils around the heart,
    Oh! who hath power of charming?
It will not list to wisdom's lore,
    Nor music's voice can lure it;
But there it stings for evermore
    The soul that must endure it.

George Noel Gordon, Lord Byron (1788–1824)

THE CONCLUSION OF THE MATTER
(See Ecclesiastes 12.13)

Fear God – obey his just decrees,
And do it hand, and heart, and knees;
For after all our utmost care
There's nought like penitence and prayer.

Then weigh the balance in your mind,
Look forward, not one glance behind;
Let no foul fiend retard your pace,
Hosanna! Thou hast won the race.

Christopher Smart (1722–71)

WISDOM
(Proverbs 8.22–31)

Ere God had built the mountains,
Or raised the fruitful hills;
Before he fill'd the fountains
That feed the running rills;
In me, from everlasting,
The wonderful I AM,
Found pleasures never-wasting,
And Wisdom is my name.

When, like a tent to dwell in,
He spread the skies abroad,
And swathed about the swelling
Of Ocean's mighty flood;
He wrought by weight and measure,
And I was with him then:
Myself the Father's pleasure,
And mine, the sons of men,

Thus Wisdom's words discover
Thy glory and thy grace,
Thou everlasting lover
Of our unworthy race!
Thy gracious eye survey'd us
Ere stars were seen above;
In wisdom thou hast made us,
And died for us in love.

And couldst thou be delighted
With creatures such as we,
Who, when we saw thee, slighted
And nail'd thee to a tree?

Unfathomable wonder,
And mystery divine!
The voice that speaks in thunder,
Says, 'Sinner, I am thine!'

William Cowper (1731–1800)

UPON THE PISMIRE
(Proverbs 6.6–11)

Must we unto the pismire go to school,
　To learn of her in summer to provide
For winter next ensuing. Man's a fool,
　Or silly ants would not be made his guide.
But, sluggard, is it not a shame for thee
　To be outdone by pismires? Pr'ythee hear:
Their works, too, will thy condemnation be
　When at the judgment-seat thou shalt appear.
But since thy God doth bid thee to her go,
　Obey, her ways consider, and be wise;
The piss-ant tell thee will what thou must do,
　And set the way to life before thine eyes.

John Bunyan

pismire: old term for ant

THE ROSE OF SHARON

Sharon the garden of the world,
　the Pride of Palestine;
Whose Natural soil more Glory bore
　than Solomon could resign;
Could ne'er produce so sweet a Rose
　as I will be to Thee.
So fair a Lily never grew,
　Sharon must stoop to Me.

O Blessed Jesus, dost thou say,
    who'll have a Rose so sweet!
Who will refuse our Sharon's Rose,
    that knows its fragrant scent?
Upon the Cross thou was Distilled,
    we taste in Distillation,
The sweetness of the absent Rose,
    by faith and acceptation.

Thou art a Rose, my Soul's repose,
    O let me never be,
My Dearest Lord, a Thorn to thee,
    who art so sweet to me.
Thou art the Lily of the Vale,
    a matchless Purity.
And I will sing thy Praise since thou
    dost in my bosom lie.

Benjamin Keach (1640–1704)

RISE UP, MY LOVE
(Song of Songs 2)

Rise up, my Love, my fairest one,
    Make no delay
Now winter's utmost blast hath blown
    Himself away.

The cloudy curtain's drawn aside
    To free the light;
No drop is left, pure Heaven to hide
    From thy full sight.

The cheerly earth doth, as she may,
    Reflect heaven's face
With flowery constellations gay
    In every place.

Our birds sit tuning their soft throats
  The angels' quire
To echo back: the turtle's notes
  With them conspire.

The teeming fig-trees new-born brood
  Abroad appear,
Vines and young grapes breathe out a good
  And wholesome air.

All sweets invite us to lay down
  Our dull delay;
Rise up, my Love, my fairest one,
  And come away.
   Joseph Beaumont (1616–99)

turtle: turtle-dove

PASSING AWAY, SAITH THE WORLD
(See Song of Songs 2.10–13)

Passing away, saith the World, passing away:
Chances, beauty and youth, sapp'd day by day:
Thy life never continueth in one stay.
Is the eye waxen dim, is the dark hair changing to grey
That hath won neither laurel nor bay?
I shall clothe myself in Spring and bud in May:
Thou, root-stricken, shalt not rebuild thy decay
On my bosom for aye.
Then I answer'd: Yea.

Passing away, saith my Soul, passing away:
With its burden of fear and hope, of labour and play,
Hearken what the past doth witness and say:
Rust in thy gold, a moth is in thine array,
A canker is in thy bud, thy leaf must decay.
At midnight, at cockcrow, at morning, one certain day
Lo, the Bridegroom shall come and shall not delay:
Watch thou and pray.
Then I answer'd: Yea.

Passing away, saith my God, passing away:
Winter passeth after the long delay:
New grapes on the vine, new figs on the tender spray,
Turtle calleth turtle in Heaven's May.
Though I tarry, wait for Me, trust Me, watch and pray.
Arise, come away, night is past and lo it is day,
My love, My sister, My spouse, thou shalt hear Me say.
Then I answer'd: Yea.

Christina Rossetti (1830–94)

turtle: turtle-dove

CHRIST, MY BELOVED

Christ, my Beloved which still doth feed
  Among the flowers, having delight
   Among his faithful lilies,
Doth take great care for me indeed,
  And I again with all my might
   Will do what so his will is.

My Love in me and I in him,
  Conjoined by love, who still abide
   Among the faithful lilies
'Till day do break, and truth do dim
  All shadows dark and cause them slide,
   According as his will is.

William Baldwin (sixteenth century)

CHRIST TO HIS SPOUSE

Lo, thou, my love, art fair;
  Myself hath made thee so:
Yea, thou art fair indeed,
Wherefore thou shalt not need
In beauty to despair;
For I accept thee so,
  For fair.

For fair, because thine eyes
    Are like the culvers' white,
Whose simpleness in deed
All others do exceed:
Thy judgement wholly lies
In true sense of sprite
    Most wise.

William Baldwin

culver: woodpigeon

IN PRAISE OF HIS BELOVED
(Song of Songs 4.1–7)

How beautiful you are
my delectable maiden
O daughter of delight.

Behind your frail veil's wispy thread
your timid eyes retreat,
their coy and bashful glances
your nervous invitation give.
Your flitting lashes.
the trembling fluttering of a dove.

Your glistening hair, its glossy locks
your motion whirls, their glowing curls
they twist and turn with dancing undulation,
the distant flocks of flowing goats
which ripple down the verdant slopes.

Your fresh white teeth
so clean, so smooth,
like skin of sheep so closely shorn
and washed and bleached.
Each with matching set of twins
gleaming in perfect symmetry,
and none without its partner.

Your fulsome shapely lips
a silky scarlet band
around your comely mouth,
which frames your mellowed speech.

Your veil's fine web of tracery
its gossamer of lace,
their soft fine shadow cast
upon the contours of your face.
Your temple's gentle roundness,
your curving downy cheeks
entraced with mesh so delicate,
an image of a pomegranate
of rosy hue and membranes soft.

Your stately neck bedecked
by layered rows of beads,
secure and strong, impregnable,
like David's royal tower,
majestic with its trophies,
the spoils of ancient wars.
Its serried ranks of shiny shields,
adorn its panelled walls.

Your shy twin breasts
two timid fawns to stroke
which gently graze among the cusps,
the lips of fragrant lilies.

Until the gleam of nature's morn,
until the early hours of dawn
when sun's first ray does chase away
the shadows of the night,
I'll run and spring on mountain heights
on contours of the countryside,
her fresh and fragrant slopes.

Wholly delectable you are, my darling,
flawless in your unique perfection.

Tom Gledhill (b. 1942)

ANOTHER DREAM OF FRUSTRATION

(Song of Songs 5.2–8)

Restless sleeping in the night
thoughts in motion, never ceasing,
troubled dreaming,
turning, churning through the night.

Knock! Knock! In the darkness of the night.
What intruding plight is this?
Knock! Knock! Knocking.
Who is there?
Beating in the midnight air?

Slowly waking, eyelids rubbing,
surely not my lover late
at the portals of my gate.
Urgent whispers, 'Quick, it's me.
Let me in! I'm soaked with dew,
Glistening drops, dripping from my curly locks.
Quick, let me in, my precious dove.
My flawless one, my only love.'

Knock! Knock! Just who is this?
Am I dreaming? Is it him?
Should I rise to let him in?
Methinks I would my lover tease.
Just who is he that I should please his every whim?
Why not delay his coming in
and play my tricks and leave him standing,
dripping, shivering on the landing.

'My lover dear, just keep at bay,
I've taken off my negligée.
Too late to put my wrapper on
and soil again my dainty feet,
to rise and let you in again,
into my cosy chamber.'

He put his hand through at the latch;
I sensed the thrill, my heart did catch
with pounding jolt.
I sprang to let my lover in,
my fragrant fingers at the bolt.

I opened wide to let him in
But O despair, no-one there!
Nothing but the midnight air.
He'd turned and gone,
He'd taken flight,
into the darkness of the night.

I nearly died,
My mind went blank,
my heavy heart with sickness sank
in aweful black dejection.
Into the city streets I ran,
searching here, calling there.
The eerie empty square,
mockingly replied, with footsteps hollow echoing.
With urgent desperation, I sought my absent lover.
I sought but did not find him.
But they found me,
the stolid watchmen of the night,
the city walls patrolling,
stern guardians of morality.
They took me for a wandering girl
of doubtful reputation.
They beat me, bruised me,
they stripped me of my outer dress
and left me crying in distress.

O Daughters of Jerusalem,
I put you under oath.
I beg you not to tell my lover
that I'm smitten with an illness,
a sickness of the heart,
that sent me on a wild goose chase,
this crazy escapade.

Tom Gledhill

HIS EYES ARE LIKE THE EYES OF DOVES

(Song of Songs 5.12)

I'll tell you farther, that if such
    A Person you shall see,
Whose Eyes like Doves are wash't with Milk
    and Water this is he?
He hath a killing Eye, 'twill Pierce
    through Adamantine Ears;
And wound a Rock but with a look,
    and melt it into Tears.

Eyes that are clear and fitly set,
    that can see all things past,
and all things present and to come,
    as long as Time shall last:
Whose Eyes are Pure, Holy and Chaste,
    never defiled with Sin;
That never was in the least Promp't
    to take foul Objects in.

If such a One you meet, whose Eyes
    like Flames, and lamps of Fire
Strikes Dead, and yet gives Life thereby,
    'tis he that I desire?
This is the Man I seek, and praise,
    All-seeing, and All-Eye:
Tell him, if such a one you meet,
    'tis for his love, I die!

Benjamin Keach

adamantine ears: determinedly resistant to listening

A DIVINE RAPTURE

E'en like two little bank-dividing brooks,
That wash the pebbles with their wanton streams,
And having ranged and search'd a thousand nooks,
Meet both at length in silver-breasted Thames,
Where in a greater current they conjoin:
So I my Best-belovèd's am; so He is mine.

E'en so we met; and after long pursuit,
E'en so we joined; we both became entire;
No need for either to renew a suit,
For I was flax, and he was flames of fire:
Our firm-united souls did more than twine;
So I my Best-belovèd's am; so He is mine.

If all those glittering Monarchs, that command
The servile quarters of this earthly ball,
Should tender in exchange their shares of land,
I would not change my fortunes for them all:
Their wealth is but a counter to my coin:
The world's but theirs; but my Belovèd's mine.

Francis Quarles

THE
PROPHETS
(Isaiah to Malachi)

WE ARE THE CLAY, AND THOU
OUR POTTER
(Isaiah 64.8)

My Potter from above,
Clay in Thy hands I am,
Mould me into the form of love,
And stamp with Thy new name:
Thy name is holiness;
Now on this heart of mine
The mark indelible impress,
The purity divine.

Charles Wesley (1707–88)

THE JOY OF THE NATIONS
(Isaiah 2.2–6)

Behold! The mountain of the Lord
    In latter days shall rise
On mountain tops above the hills,
    And draw the wond'ring eyes.

To this the joyful nations round,
    All tribes and tongues shall flow;
Up to the hill of God, they'll say,
    And to his house we'll go.

The beam that shines from Sion hill
    Shall lighten ev'ry land;
The King who reigns in Salem's tow'rs
    Shall all the world command.

Among the nations he shall judge;
    His judgments truth shall guide;
His sceptre shall protect the just,
    And quell the sinner's pride.

No strife shall rage, nor hostile feuds
    Disturb those peaceful years;
To ploughshares men shall beat their swords,
    To pruning-hooks their spears.

No longer hosts encount'ring hosts
    Shall crowds of slain deplore;
They hang the trumpet in the hall
    And study war no more.

Come then, O house of Jacob! Come
    To worship at this shrine;
And, walking in the light of God,
    With holy beauties shine.

Michael Bruce

HERE AM I; SEND ME
(Isaiah 6.8)

Ah, woe is me, immersed in sin,
A man of lips and life unclean!
How shall I with Thy message run,
Or preach the pardoning God unknown?
Unless my God vouchsafe to cheer
His guilty trembling messenger,
My fears disperse, my sins remove,
And purge me by the fire of love!

O wouldst Thou touch my lips once more,
The comfort of Thy grace restore,
Assure me, Lord, that mine Thou art,
And stamp forgiveness on my heart;
Then should I in my Jesu's name
Glad tidings of great joy proclaim,
Of grace, which every soul may find,
And glory bought for all mankind.
Charles Wesley

BABYLON
(See Isaiah 13)

Bow, daughter of Babylon, bow thee to dust!
Thine heart shall be quelled, and thy pride shall be crushed:
Weep, Babylon, weep! for thy splendour is past;
And they come like the storm in the day of the blast.

Howl, desolate Babylon, lost one and lone!
And bind thee in sackcloth – for where is thy throne?
Like a winepress in wrath will I trample thee down,
And rend from thy temples the pride of thy crown.

Though thy streets be a hundred, thy gates be all brass,
Yet thy proud ones of war shall be withered like grass;
Thy gates shall be broken, thy strength be laid low,
And thy streets shall resound to the shouts of the foe!

Though thy chariots of power on thy battlements bound
And the grandeur of waters encompass thee round;
Yet thy walls shall be shaken, thy waters shall fail,
Thy matrons shall shriek, and thy king shall be pale.

The terrible day of thy fall is at hand,
When my rage shall ascend on the face of thy land;
The lances are pointed, the keen sword is bared,
The shields are anointed, the helmets prepared.

I call upon Cyrus! He comes from afar
And the armies of nations are gathered to war;
With the blood of thy children his path shall be red,
And the bright sun of conquest shall blaze o'er his head.

Thou glory of kingdoms! thy princes are drunk,
But their loins shall be loosed, and their hearts shall be sunk;
They shall crouch to the dust, and be counted as slaves,
At the roll of his wheels, like the rushing of waves!

For I am the Lord, who have mightily spanned
The breadth of the heavens, and the sea and the land;
And the mountains shall flow at my presence, and earth
Shall reel to and fro in the glance of my wrath!

Your proud domes of cedar on earth shall be thrown
And the rank grass shall wave o'er the lonely hearthstone;
And your sons and your sires and your daughters shall bleed
By the barbarous hands of the murdering Mede!

I will sweep ye away in destruction and death,
As the whirlwind that scatters the chaff with its breath;
And the fanes of your gods shall be sprinkled with gore,
And the course of your streams shall be heard of no more!

There the wandering Arab shall ne'er pitch his tent,
But the beasts of the desert shall wail and lament;
In their desolate houses the dragons shall lie,
And the satyrs shall dance, and the bitterns shall cry!
Alfred Lord Tennyson (1809–92)

THE RANSOMED OF THE LORD
RETURN WITH JOY
(Isaiah 35 paraphrased)

The wilderness and dry land sings
As each becomes the place of springs
Where fountains play and streamlets flow
And fairest flowers shall freely grow,
Gold crocuses and Sharon's Rose
Whose mystic petals each disclose
The beauty of the Son of God
Who once himself this desert trod.

The hills of Lebanon shall shine
With glory of his Light Divine,
And he who looks on high shall see
Mount Carmel clothed with Majesty.
The glory of the Lord shall be
Revealed in Awesome purity.
To those who come with trembling knee
He says 'Fear not for I am he
Who by my Spirit set you free.
Reach out all you who trembling stand
And take my loving nail-pierced hand.
To those I say of fearful heart
"I am your God, there is no part
For craven fear and wond'rings vain
I am your God who comes to Reign!" '

Then blind eyes shall be opened wide
As he the Bridegroom greets the Bride,
Deaf ears unstopped shall hear his Voice
And hearing him their hearts rejoice!
With joy the loosened tongues shall sing
Fresh praises to their Heavenly King.

The wilderness and dry land sings
As each becomes a place of springs.
The burning sand becomes a pool
Of limpid waters crystal cool
The haunt of jackals changed by Grace

Shall now be called a Resting Place.
Dry Grass becomes fresh green and lush
With swaying reed and piping rush.
A Highway he has builded there
To tread upon that Holy round
Except the Ransomed of the Lord who've found
The Living Way, as Sons of God:
Redemption in the Saviour's Blood.
No prowling lion or ravenous beast
Shall there molest the very least
Of all God's children as they tread
The Pilgrim Way that he has led.

Then all the World shall greet this Dawn,
The Ransomed of the Lord return
Upon the loved and Ancient Ways
To Zion, singing loud his Praise.
For lo! He Reigns the King of Kings
Now Risen with Healing in his Wings
Sorrow and sighing flee away
Like desert mists at break of day
Their heads raised high, each Pilgrim sings
'All glory to the King of Kings'.

David J. Payne (b. 1931)

THE HEAVENS ARE SINGING
(Based on echoes of Isaiah 44 and 45)

The heavens are singing, are singing and praising,
    The depths of the earth and the mountains rejoice;
the trees and the forests are raising, are raising
the song of creation in thunderous voice;
    for God has redeemed us,
    redeemed us and bought us,
remembered his people, and made us his choice!

The sun in his rising, his rising and setting,
    the stars in their courses, their Maker proclaim.
We only, his children, forgetting, forgetting,

the love of the Father, have turned to our shame;
    yet God has redeemed us,
    redeemed us and bought us,
remembered his people, and called us by name!

For he is the Father, the Father who made us,
who founded and fashioned the earth and the sky;
who stooped from his glory to aid us, to aid us
when yet we were sinners deserving to die;
    our God has redeemed us,
    redeemed us and bought us,
remembered his people, and lifted us high!

O Father eternal, eternally living,
Resplendent in glory, the Lord on his throne,
We praise and adore you, forgiving, forgiving,
None other beside you, in mercy alone;
    For God has redeemed us,
    Redeemed us and bought us,
Remembered his people, and made us his own!

Timothy Dudley-Smith

THE DIVINE AMBASSADOR
(Isaiah 42)

Behold th' Ambassador divine
    Descending from above,
To publish to mankind the law
    Of everlasting love!

On him in rich effusion pour'd
    The heavenly dew descends;
And truth divine he shall reveal,
    To earth's remotest ends.

No trumpet sound at his approach
    Shall strike the wondering ears;
But still and gentle breathe the voice
    In which the God appears.

By his kind hand the shaken reed
　　Shall raise its falling frame;
The dying embers shall revive,
　　And kindle to a flame.

The onward progress of his zeal
　　Shall never know decline,
Till foreign lands and distant isles
　　Receive the law divine.

He who spread forth the arch of Heaven,
　　And bade the planets roll,
Who laid the basis of the earth,
　　And form'd the human soul.

Thus saith the Lord – 'Thee have I sent
　　A Prophet from the sky,
Wide o'er the nations to proclaim
　　The message from on high.

'Before thy face the shades of death
　　Shall take to sudden flight,
The people who in darkness dwell
　　Shall hail a glorious light.

'The gates of brass shall 'sunder burst,
　　The iron fetters fall;
The promised jubilee of Heaven
　　Appointed rise o'er all.

'And lo! Presaging thy approach
　　The Heathen temples shake,
And trembling in forsaken fanes
　　The fabled idols quake.

'I am Jehovah! I am one!
　　My name shall now be known;
No idol shall usurp my praise,
　　Nor mount into my throne.'

Lo! Former scenes, predicted once,
  Conspicuous rise to view;
And future scenes, predicted now,
  Shall be accomplished too.

Now sing a new song to the Lord,
  Let earth his praise resound;
Ye who upon the ocean dwell,
  And fill the isles around.

Let Kedar's wilderness afar
  Lift up the lonely voice;
And let the tenants of the rock
  With accent rude rejoice.

O from the streams of distant lands
  Unto Jehovah sing!
And joyful from the mountain tops
  Shout to the Lord the King.

Let all combined with one accord
  Jehovah's glories raise,
Till in remotest bounds of earth
  The nations sound his praise.

Michael Bruce

I HAVE GRAVEN THEE UPON
THE PALMS OF MY HANDS
(Isaiah 49.16)

Engraven with an iron pen
My name upon Thy hands is seen:
Lord, with Thy love's acutest dart
Engrave Thy name upon my heart.

Charles Wesley

MEDITATION TWELVE

(Who is this that cometh from Edom, with dyed garments from Bozrah?
this that is glorious in his apparel, travelling in the greatness of
his strength? I that speak in righteousness, mighty to save —
Isaiah 63.1)

This quest rapped at my ears broad golden doors
    Who's this that comes from Edom in this shine,
In dyed robes from Bozrah? this more o'er
    All glorious in's apparel: all divine?
    Then through that wicket rushed this gust there gave:
    It's I that right do speak, mighty to save.

I threw through Zion's lattice then an eye
    Which spied one like a lump of glory pure:
Nay, clothes of gold buttoned with pearls do lie
    Like rags, or shoeclouts unto his he wore.
    Heaven's curtains blanched with sun, and stars of light
    Are black as sackcloth to his garments bright.

One shining sun gilding the skies with light,
    Benights all candles with their flame
So doth the glory of this robe benight
    Ten thousand suns at once ten thousand ways.
    For every third therein's dyed with the shine
    Of all, and each the attributes divine.

The sweetest breath, the sweetest violet
    Rose, or carnation ever did gust out,
Is but a foist to that perfume beset
    In thy apparel steaming round about.
    But is this so? My puling soul then pine
    In love until this lovely one be thine.

Pluck back the curtains, back the window shuts
    Through Zion's agate window take a view,
How Christ in pinked robes from Bozrah puts,
    Comes glorious in's apparel forth to woo.
    Oh! if his glory ever kiss thine eye,
    Thy love will soon enchanted be thereby.

Then grieve, my soul, thy vessel is so small,
    And holds no more for such a lovely he.
That strength's so little, love scarce acts at all
      That sight's so dim, doth scarce him lovely see.
      Grieve, grieve, my soul, thou shouldst so pimp
      Now such a price is here presented thee.

All sight's too little sight enough to make
    All strength's too little love enough to rear,
All vessels are too small to hold or take
      Enough love up for such a lovely dear.
      How little to this little's then thy all,
      For him whose beauty saith all love's too small?

My lovely one, I fain would love thee much,
    But all my love is none at all I see;
Oh! let thy beauty give a glorious touch
      Upon my heart, and melt to love all me.
      Lord, melt me all up into love for thee,
      Whose loveliness excels what love can be.

    Edward Taylor (c. 1645–1729)

wicket: small opening; **shoeclouts**: leather patches; **puling**: whinging, or crying plaintively; **pimp**: pander to lust or immoral impulse

FROM THE LAMENTATIONS OF JEREMY, FOR THE MOST PART ACCORDING TO TREMELLIUS
(Lamentations 1)

How sits the city, late most populous,
Thus solitary, and like a widow thus?
Amplest of nations, queen of provinces
She was, who now thus tributary is?

Still in the night she weeps, and her tears fall
Down by her cheeks along, and none of all
Her lovers comfort her; perfidiously
Her friends have dealt, and now are enemy.

Unto great bondage, and afflictions,
Judah is captive led; those nations
With whom she dwells, no place of rest afford;
In straits she meets her persecutors' sword.

Empty are the gates of Sion, and her ways
Mourn, because none come to her solemn days.
Her priests do groan, her maids are comfortless;
And she's unto herself a bitterness.

Her foes are grown her head, and live at peace,
Because, when her transgressions did increase,
The Lord struck her with sadness; the enemy
Doth strive her children to captivity.

From Sion's daughter is all beauty gone;
Like harts which seek for pasture, and find none,
Her princes are; and now before the foe
Which still pursues them, without strength they go.

Now in their days of tears, Jerusalem
– Her men slain by the foe, none succouring them –
Remembers what of old she esteemed most,
Whiles her foes laugh at her, for what she hath lost.

Jerusalem hath sinn'd, therefore is she
Removed, as women in uncleanness be;
Who honour'd, scorn her, for her foulness they
Have seen; herself doth groan, and turn away.

Her foulness in her skirts was seen, yet she
Rememb'd not her end; miraculously
Therefore she fell, none comforting; behold,
O Lord, my affliction, for the foe grows bold.

Upon all things where her delight hath been,
The foe hath stretch'd his hand, for she hath seen
Heathen, whom thou command'st should not do so,
Into her holy sanctuary go.

And all her people groan, and seek for bread;
And they have given, only to be fed,

All precious things, wherein their pleasure lay;
How cheap I'm grown, O Lord, behold, and weigh.

All this concerns not you, who pass by me;
O see, and mark if any sorrow be
Like to my sorrow, which Jehovah hath
Done to me in the day of his fierce wrath?

That fire, which by himself is governed,
He hath cast from heaven on my bones, and spread
A net before my feet, and me o'erthrown,
And made me languish all the day alone.

His hand hath of my sins framèd a yoke
Which wreathed, and cast upon my neck, hath broke
My strength; the Lord unto those enemies
Hath given me, from whom I cannot rise.

He under foot hath trodden in my sight
My strong men; he did company accite
To break my young men; he the winepress hath
Trod upon Judah's daughter in his wrath.

For these things do I weep; mine eye, mine eye
Casts water out; for he which should be nigh
To comfort me, is now departed far;
The foe prevails, forelorn my children are.

There's none, though Sion do stretch out her hand
To comfort her; it is the Lord's command
That Jacob's foes girt him; Jerusalem
Is as an unclean woman amongst them.

But yet the Lord is just, and righteous still;
I have rebell'd against his holy will;
O hear all people, and my sorrow see,
My maids, my young men in captivity.

I called for my lovers then, but they
Deceived me, and my priests, and elders lay
Dead in the city; for they sought for meat
Which should refresh their souls, and none could get.

Because I am in straits, Jehovah, see!
My heart o'erturn'd, my bowels muddy be;
Because I have rebell'd so much, as fast
The sword without, as death within, doth waste.

Of all which here I mourn, none comforts me;
My foes have heard my grief, and glad they be,
That thou hast done it; but thy promised day
Will come, when, as I suffer, so shall they.

Let all their wickedness appear to thee;
Do unto them, as thou hast done to me,
For all my sins; the sighs which I have had
Are very many, and my heart is sad.

John Donne (1572–1631)

accite: excite, summon

BEYOND ALL MORTAL PRAISE
(Based on Daniel 2.20–23)

Beyond all mortal praise
God's Name be ever blest,
unsearchable his ways,
his glory manifest;
　　from his high throne
　　in power and might
　　by wisdom's light
　　he rules alone.

Our times are in his hand
to whom all flesh is grass,
while as their Maker planned
the changing seasons pass.
　　He orders all:
　　before his eyes
　　earth's empires rise,
　　her kingdoms fall.

He gives to humankind,
dividing as he will,
all powers of heart and mind,
of spirit, strength and skill:
    nor dark nor night
    but must lay bare
    its secrets, where
    he dwells in light.

To God the only Lord,
our fathers' God, be praise;
his holy Name adored
through everlasting days.
    His mercies trace
    in answered prayer,
    in love and care,
    and gifts of grace.

Timothy Dudley-Smith

NEBUCHADNEZZAR
(See Daniel 3)

My body is weary to death of my mischievous brain;
I am weary forever and ever of being brave;
Therefore I crouch on my knees while the cool white rain
Curves the clover over my head like a wave.

The stem and the frosty seed of the grass are ripe;
I have devoured their strength; I have drunk them deep;
And the dandelion is gall in a thin green pipe;
But the clover is honey and sun and the smell of sleep.

Elinor Wylie (1885–1928)

BELSHAZZAR'S LETTER

Belshazzar had a letter, –
He never had but one;
Belshazzar's correspondent
Concluded and begun
In that immortal copy
The conscience of us all
Can read without its glosses
On revelation's wall.

Emily Dickinson

JONAH FLEES FROM GOD
(Jonah 1.1–16)

Now unto Jonah, old Amittai's son,
Thus did the word of the Almighty come,
And said, Arise, go thou forthwith and cry
'Gainst that great city Nineveh; for why,
The sins thereof are come up in my sight.
But he arose, that he to Tarshish might
Flee from God's presence; and went down and found
A ship at Joppa unto Tarshish bound:
He paid the fare, and with them went on board
For Tarshish, from the presence of the Lord.

But the Almighty a great wind did raise,
And sent a mighty tempest on the seas,
So that the ship was likely to be broken.
Then were the mariners with horror stricken;
And to his God they cried every one;
And overboard was the ship's lading thrown
To lighten it: but down into the ship
Was Jonah gone, and there lay fast asleep.

So to him came the master and did say,
What meanest thou, O sleeper! rise and pray
Unto thy God, and he perhaps will hear,
And save us from the danger that we fear.
Then said they to each other, Come let's try,

By casting lots, on whom the fault doth lie,
In bringing all this evil now upon us.
So they cast lots, and the lot fell on Jonas.

Then said they, We entreat thee let us know,
For whose cause we this evil undergo,
Whence comest thou? What is thine occupation?
What countryman art thou? And of what nation?
And unto them himself he did declare,
And said, I am an Hebrew, and do fear
The living Lord, the God of heaven, who
Alone hath made the sea and dry land too.

Then were the men exceedingly afraid;
And, wherefore hast thou done this thing? they said:
(For they did understand he did forego
God's presence, for himself had told them so.)
What shall we do unto thee, then they said,
That so the raging of the sea be stay'd?
(For it did rage and foam.) Take me, said he,
And cast me overboard into the sea;
So shall the sea be calm, for on my score
I know it is, that thus the waves do roar.

Nevertheless they rowed hard to gain
The land, but all their labour was in vain;
So much against them did the tempest beat.
Wherefore they the Almighty did entreat,
And said, We do beseech thee, and we pray,
O Lord, that thou would'st not upon us lay
The charge of guiltless blood, nor let it be,
That now we perish, on th' account that we
Take this man's life away; for thou alone
As it hath pleased thee, O Lord, hast done.

So they took Jonah up, and to the seas
Committed him, then did the tempest cease.
Then did the dread of the great God on high,
Seize on the mariners exceedingly.
And they did offer up a sacrifice,
And vowed vows unto the Lord likewise.

John Bunyan

RELUCTANT PROPHET

Both were dwellers
in deep places (one
in the dark bowels
of ships and great fish
and wounded pride.
The other
in the silvery belly
of the seas.) Both
heard God saying
'Go!'
but the whale
did as he was told.

Luci Shaw (b. 1928)

THE RIBS AND TERRORS
(See Jonah 2)

The ribs and terrors in the whale,
    Arched over me a dismal gloom,
While all God's sun-lit waves rolled by,
    And lift me to a deeper doom.

I saw the opening maw of hell,
With endless pains and sorrows there;
Which none but they that feel can tell –
    Oh, I was plunging to despair.

In black distress, I called my God,
    When I could scarce believe him mine,
He bowed his ear to my complaints –
    No more the whale did me confine.

With speed he flew to my relief,
    As on a radiant dolphin borne;
Awful, yet bright, as lightning shone
    The face of my Deliverer God.

My song for ever shall record
    That terrible, that joyful hour;
I give the glory to my God,
    His all the mercy and the power.

Herman Melville (1819–91)

REND YOUR HEARTS
(Joel 2.13–17)

Rend your hearts, not your garments, my people;
Return to the Lord God of grace.
Slow to anger and rich in compassion,
He will rescue the meek from disgrace.

Blow the trumpet in Zion, my people;
Turn to fasting and seeking God's face.
Call the elders and people and children
To assemble at God's holy place.

Weep for covenant mercy, my people;
Let not faith disappear without trace.
Rend your hearts, not your garments, my people,
And return to the Lord God of grace.

Norman Fraser (b. 1962)

AS A SPRING POURS OUT WATER
(Joel 2.28–29)

As a spring pours out water
So will I pour out my Spirit on all flesh.
As a spring pours out water
So will I pour out words of wisdom on your offspring.
As a spring pours out water
So will I pour out dreams into the night spaces and heart places
    of old men.

As a spring pours out water
So will I pour out visions beyond the sharpest sight of warriors.
As a spring pours out water
So will I pour out my Spirit on my willing servants in those days.
Until my Spirit pours out of them
As from a spring of living water.

Norman Fraser

THE
GOSPELS AND ACTS

A God and yet a man,
A maid and yet a mother:
Wit wonders what wit can
Conceive this or the other.

A God and can he die?
A dead man, can he live?
What wit can well reply?
What reason reason give?

God, Truth itself, doth teach it.
Man's wit sinks too far under
By reason's power to reach it:
Believe and leave to wonder.

Anon. (fifteenth century)

AT THE MANGER MARY SINGS

O shut your bright eyes that mine must endanger
With their watchfulness; protected by its shade
Escape from my care: what can you discover
From my tender look but how to be afraid?
Love can but confirm the more it would deny.
   Close your bright eye.

Sleep. What have you learned from the womb that bore you
But an anxiety your Father cannot feel?
Sleep. What will the flesh that I gave do for you,
Or my mother love, but tempt you from His will?
Why was I chosen to teach His Son to weep?
   Little One, sleep.

Dream. In human dreams earth ascends to Heaven
Where no one need pray nor ever feel alone.
In your first few hours of life here, O have you
Chosen already what death must be your own?
How soon will you start on the Sorrowful Way?
   Dream while you may.

W. H. Auden (1907–73)

GO TELL IT ON THE MOUNTAINS

When I was a learner,
I sought both night and day,
I ask the Lord to aid me,
An' he show me the way.

He made me a watchman,
Upon the city wall,
An' if I am a Christian,
I am the least of all.

Go tell it on the mountains,
Over the hills an' ev'rywhere,
Go tell it on the mountains,
Our Jesus Christ is born.

Traditional Black American Spiritual

MARY'S SONG

Blue homespun and the bend of my breast
keep warm this small hot naked star
fallen to my arms. (Rest . . .
you who have had so far
to come.) Now nearness satisfies
the body of God sweetly. Quiet he lies
whose vigour hurled
a universe. He sleeps
whose eyelids have not closed before.
His breath (so slight it seems
no breath at all) once ruffled the dark deeps
to sprout a world.
Charmed by dove's voices, the whisper of straw,
he dreams,
hearing no music from his other spheres.
Breath, mouth, ears, eyes
he is curtailed
who overflowed all skies,
all years.
Older than eternity, now he
is new. Now native to earth as I am, nailed
to my poor planet, caught that I might be free,
blind in my womb to know my darkness ended,
brought to this birth
for me to be new-born,
and for him to see me mended
I must see him torn.

Luci Shaw (b. 1928)

THE SONG OF SIMEON
(Luke 2.25–33)

Just and devout old Simeon liv'd
    To him it was reveal'd,
That Christ, the Lord, his eyes should see
    Ere death his eyelids seal'd.

For this consoling gift of Heav'n
    To Isr'el's fallen state,
From year to year with patient hope
    The aged saint did wait.

Nor did he wait in vain; for, lo!
    Revolving years brought round,
In season due, the happy day,
    Which all his wishes crown'd.

When Jesus, to the temple brought
    By Mary's pious care,
As Heav'n's appointed rites requir'd,
    To God was offer'd there.

Simeon into those sacred courts
    A heav'nly impulse drew:
He saw the Virgin hold her son,
    And straight his Lord he knew.

With holy joy upon his face
    The good old father smil'd;
Then fondly in his wither'd arms
    He clasp'd the promis'd child.

And while he held the heav'n-born Babe,
    Ordain'd to bless mankind,
Thus spoke with earnest look, and heart
    Exulting, yet resign'd:

Now, Lord! According to thy word,
    Let me in peace depart;
Mine eyes have thy salvation seen
    And gladness fills my heart.

At length my arms embrace my Lord,
    Now let their vigour cease;
At last my eyes my Saviour see,
    Now let them close in peace.

This great salvation, long prepar'd,
    And now disclos'd to view,
Hath prov'd thy love was constant still,
    And promises were true.

That Sun I now behold, whose light
Shall heathen darkness chase,
And rays of brightest glory pour
Around thy chosen race.

Michael Bruce

JOURNEY OF THE MAGI

'A cold coming we had of it,
Just the worst time of the year
For a journey, and such a long journey:
The ways deep and the weather sharp,
The very dead of winter.'
And the camels galled, sore-footed, refractory,
Lying down in the melting snow.
There were times we regretted
The summer palaces on slopes, the terraces,
And the silken girls bringing sherbet.
Then the camel men cursing and grumbling
And running away, and wanting their liquor and women,
And the night-fires going out, and the lack of shelters,
And the cities hostile and the towns unfriendly
And the villages dirty and charging high prices:
A hard time we had of it.
At the end we preferred to travel all night,
Sleeping in snatches,
With the voices singing in our ears, saying
That this was all folly.

Then at dawn we came down to a temperate valley,
Wet, below the snow line, smelling of vegetation,
With a running stream and a water-mill beating the darkness,
And three trees on the low sky.
And an old white horse galloped away in the meadow.
Then we came to a tavern with vine-leaves over the lintel,
Six hands at an open door dicing for pieces of silver,
And feet kicking the empty wine-skins.
But there was no information, and so we continued
And arrived at evening, not a moment too soon
Finding the place; it was (you may say) satisfactory.

All this was a long time ago, I remember,
And I would do it again, but set down
This set down
This: were we led all that way for
Birth or Death? There was a Birth, certainly,
We had evidence and no doubt. I had seen birth and death,
But had thought they were different; this Birth was
Hard and bitter agony for us, like Death, our death.
We returned to our places, these Kingdoms,
But no longer at ease here, in the old dispensation,
With an alien people clutching their gods.
I should be glad of another death.

T. S. Eliot (1888–1965)

TWO POEMS FOR THE EPIPHANY

1
'This is your road,' sang the bright nova.
'This way, this way!' celestial birds
Shrilled inside their skulls.

Their paths converged before a gaping cave,
A makeshift shelter for cattle.
The Child – vulnerable, red,
Hairless, with pulsing fontanelle –
Received the unbidden gifts.

Three kings – one, blond and frosty eyed,
Chinked the gold coins; a second, yellow,
Long fingernails sheathed in jade, was grasping
A bundle of joss-sticks; while the third
Black-skinned and curly, offered
The bitter herb that's bred from servitude.

2
Winter, a cave, the glittering
Of an unnamed star, to bring
A yellow, a red, and a black king,
With fragrant gum, with gleaming awe,
And with that bitter herb of death:
'Come,' said the wind, with icy breath.

'Come, draw near: you touch, you see
The pivot of the galaxy,
The fire that kindles the sun's core –
God's, and man's epiphany.'

John Heath-Stubbs (b. 1918)

ON JOHN THE BAPTIST
(From The Flowers of Sin)

The last and greatest herald of heaven's King,
Girt with rough skins, hies to the deserts wild,
Among that savage brood the words forth bring,
Which he than man more harmless found and mild:
His food was locusts, and what young doth spring
With honey that from virgin hives distilled;
Parched body, hollow eyes, some uncouth thing
Made him appear, long since from earth exiled.
There burst him forth: 'All ye, whose hopes rely
On God, with me amidst these deserts mourn,
Repent, repent, and from old errors turn.'
Who listened to his voice, obeyed his cry?
Only the echoes, which he made relent,
Rung from their marble caves, 'Repent, repent.'

William Drummond of Hawthornden (1585–1649)

JOHN THE BAPTIST

Racous John skilled in epiplexis
rounds the pious ears of Pharisees,
stumps the desert to raise a righteous caucus
and clear the streets of unbelief for Jesus.

The locust-honey diet makes him lithe,
the rough leather jerkin shows him humble.
His lungs are purged of cant by desert air,
his Isaianic eyes alert to wonder.

Expert Messiah-watcher, he, not fooled
by desert sharpers greedy for miracles
and promising easy kingdoms, is faithfully
awake to give the inaugural word, 'Behold!'
Eugene H. Peterson

THE FIRST TEMPTATION
(From Paradise Regained, Book One, lines 280–502)

'But, as I rose out of the laving stream,
Heaven opened her eternal doors, from whence
The Spirit descended on me like a Dove;
And last, the sum of all, my Father's voice,
Audibly heard from Heaven, pronounced me his,
Me his beloved Son, in whom alone
He was well pleased: by which I knew the time
Now full, that I no more should live obscure,
But openly begin, as best becomes
The authority which I derived from Heaven.
And now by some strong motion I am led
Into this wilderness; to what intent
I learn not yet. Perhaps I need not know;
For what concerns my knowledge God reveals.'

So spake our Morning Star, then in his rise,
And, looking round, on every side beheld
A pathless desert, dusk with horrid shades.
The way he came, not having marked return,
Was difficult, by human steps untrod;
And he still on was led, but with such thoughts
Accompanied of things past and to come
Lodged in his breast as well might recommend
Such solitude before choicest society.

Full forty days he passed – whether on hill
Sometimes, anon in shady vale, each night
Under the covert of some ancient oak
Or cedar to defend him from the dew,
Or harboured in one cave, is not revealed;
Nor tasted human food, nor hunger felt,
Till those days ended; hungered then at last
Among wild beasts. They at his sight grew mild,

Nor sleeping him nor waking harmed; his walk
The fiery serpent fled and noxious worm;
The lion and fierce tiger glared aloof.

But now an aged man in rural weeds,
Following, as seemed, the quest of some stray ewe,
Or withered sticks to gather, which might serve
Against a winter's day, when winds blow keen
To warm him wet returned from field at eve,
He saw approach; who first with curious eye
Perused him, then with words thus uttered spake: –

'Sir, what ill chance hath brought thee to this place,
So far from path or road of men, who pass
In troop or caravan? for single none
Durst ever, who returned, and dropped not here
His carcass, pined with hunger and with drought?
I ask the rather, and the more admire,
For that to me thou seemest the man whom late
Our new baptizing Prophet at the ford
Of Jordan honoured so, and called thee Son
Of God. I saw and heard, for we sometimes
Who dwell this wild, constrained by want, come forth
To town or village nigh (nighest is far),
Where aught we hear, and curious are to hear,
What happens new; fame also finds us out.'

To whom the Son of God: – 'Who brought me hither
Will bring me hence; no other guide I seek.'

'By miracle he may,' replied the swain;
'What other way I see not; for we here
Live on tough roots and stubs, to thirst inured
More than the camel, and to drink go far –
Men to much misery and hardship born.
But, if thou be the Son of God, command
That out of these hard stones be made thee bread;
So shalt thou save thyself, and us relieve
With food, whereof we wretched seldom taste.'

He ended, and the Son of God replied: –
'Think'st thou such force in bread? Is it not written
(For I discern thee other than thou seem'st),

Man lives not by bread only, but each word
Proceeding from the mouth of God, who fed
Our fathers here with manna? In the Mount
Moses was forty days, nor eat nor drank;
And forty days Eliah without food
Wandered this barren waste; the same I now.
Why dost thou, then, suggest to me distrust
Knowing who I am, as I know who thou art?'

   Whom thus answered the Arch-Fiend, now undisguised: –
"Tis true, I am that Spirit unfortunate
Who, leagued with millions more in rash revolt,
Kept not my happy station, but was driven
With them from bliss to the bottomless Deep –
Yet to that hideous place not so confined
By rigour unconniving but that oft,
Leaving my dolorous prison, I enjoy
Large liberty to round this globe of Earth,
Or range in the Air; nor from the Heaven of Heavens
Hath he excluded my resort sometimes.
I came, among the Sons of God, when he
Gave up into my hands Uzzean Job,
To prove him, and illustrate his high worth

  . . .

'Nearer acquainted, now I feel by proof
That fellowship in pain divides not smart,
Nor lightens aught each man's peculiar load;
Small consolation, then, were Man adjoined.
This wounds me most (what can it less?) that Man,
Man fallen, shall be restored, I never more.'

   To whom our Saviour sternly thus replied: –
'Deservedly thou griev'st, composed of lies
From the beginning, and in lies wilt end,
Who boast'st release from Hell, and leave to come
Into the Heaven of Heavens. Thou com'st, indeed,
As a poor miserable captive thrall
Comes to the place where he before had sat
Among the prime in splendour, now deposed,
Ejected, emptied, gazed, unpitied, shunned,

A spectacle of ruin, or of scorn,
To all the host of Heaven. The happy place
Imparts to thee no happiness, no joy –
Rather inflames thy torment, representing
Lost bliss, to thee no more communicable . . .

. . .

. . . Thou, with trembling fear,
Or like a fawning parasite, obey'st;
Then to thyself ascrib'st the truth foretold.
But this thy glory shall be soon retrenched;
No more shalt thou by oracling abuse
The Gentiles; henceforth oracles are ceased,
And thou no more with pomp and sacrifice
Shalt be enquired at Delphos or elsewhere –
At least in vain, for they shall find thee mute.
God hath now sent his living Oracle
Into the world to teach his final will,
And sends his Spirit of Truth henceforth to dwell
In pious hearts, an inward oracle
To all truth requisite for men to know.'

So spake our Saviour; but the subtle Fiend,
Though inly stung with anger and disdain,
Dissembled, and this answer smooth returned: –

'Sharply thou hast insisted on rebuke,
And urged me hard with doings which not will,
But misery, hath wrested from me. Where
Easily canst thou find one miserable,
And not inforced oft-times to part from truth,
If it may stand him more in stead to lie,
Say and unsay, feign, flatter, or abjure?
But thou art placed above me; thou art Lord;
From thee I can, and must, submiss, endure
Cheek or reproof, and glad to scape so quit.
Hard are the ways of truth, and rough to walk,
Smooth on the tongue discoursed, pleasing to the ear,
And tunable as sylvan pipe or song;
What wonder, then, if I delight to hear
Her dictates from thy mouth? most men admire

Virtue who follow not her lore. Permit me
To hear thee when I come (since no man comes),
And talk at least, though I despair to attain.
Thy Father, who is holy, wise, and pure,
Suffers the hypocrite or atheous priest
To tread his sacred courts, and minister
About his altar, handling holy things,
Praying or vowing, and vouchsafed his voice
To Balaam reprobate, a prophet yet
Inspired: disdain not such access to me.'

To whom our Saviour, with unaltered brow: –
'Thy coming hither, though I know thy scope,
I bid not, or forbid. Do as thou find'st
Permission from above; thou canst not more.'

He added not; and Satan, bowing low
His gray dissimulation, disappeared,
Into thin air diffused: for now began
Night with her sullen wing to double-shade
The desert; fowls in their clay nests were couched;
And now wild beasts came forth the woods to roam.

John Milton

TWO BROTHERS

(Jesus . . . saw two brethren . . . casting a net into the sea –
Matthew 4.18)

The schools of scribes, and courts of kings,
    The learn'd and great he passes by,
Chooses the weak and foolish things,
    His power and grace to testify;
Plain simple men his call endues
    With power and wisdom from above;
And such he still vouchsafes to use,
    Who nothing know but Jesus' love.

Charles Wesley

THE BEATITUDES
(from Matthew 5)

And Jesus, seeing the multitudes, ascended
Up to a mount, where sitting, and attended
By his disciples, he began to preach;
And on this manner following did them teach.
Blessed are all such as are poor in spirit,
For they the heavenly kingdom do inherit.
Blessed are they that mourn; for in the stead
Thereof shall comfort be administered.
Blessed are they, whose meekness doth excel:
For on the earth their portion is to dwell.
Blessed are they, who after righteousness
Hunger and thirst; for they shall it possess.
Blessed are they, for they shall mercy find,
Who to do mercifully are inclin'd.
Blessed are all such as are pure in heart;
For God his presence shall to them impart.
Blessed are they that do make peace; for why?
They shall be call'd the sons of the Most High.
Blessed are they which suffer for the sake
Of righteousness: for they of heav'n partake.
Blessed are ye, when men shall falsely speak
All kind of ill against you for my sake,
And shall revile, and persecute you sore;
Rejoice, and be exceeding glad therefore:
For your reward in heav'n will be great:
For thus of old they did the prophets treat.
Ye are the salt o' th' earth; but wherewith must
The earth be season'd when the savour's lost?
It is from thenceforth good for nothing, but
To be cast out, and trodd'n under foot.
Ye are the light o' th' world; a city set
Upon an hill cannot be hid; nor yet
Do men a candle with a bushel cover,
But set it where it lights the whole house over.
So shine your light, your good works seen thereby
Men may your heavenly Father glorify.

John Bunyan

DON'T JUDGE
(from Matthew 7)

Judge not that you may not be judg'd; for even
As you pass judgment, judgment shall be giv'n:
And with such measure as you mete to men,
It shall be measured unto you again.
And why dost thou take notice of the mote
That's in thy brother's eye; but dost not note
The beam that's in thine own? How wilt thou say
Unto thy brother, let me take away
The mote that's in thine eye, when yet 'tis plain
The beam that's in thine own doth still remain?
First cast away the beam, thou hypocrite,
From thine own eye, so shall thy clearer sight
The better be enabled to descry,
And pluck the mote out of thy brother's eye.
Give not to dogs the things that are divine,
Neither cast ye your pearls before the swine
Lest that they should their feet them trample under,
And turn upon you, and rend you asunder.
Ask, and obtain; seek, and ye shall find; do ye
Knock, and it shall be opened unto ye:
For he that seeks, shall find; that asks, obtain,
And he that knocks, shall an admittance gain.

John Bunyan

PERFECT PEACE
(Matthew 6.27)

Unprofitable all and vain,
Away this soul-distracting care!
I cannot lengthen out my span,
I cannot change a single hair;

Then let me hang upon his word
Who keeps his saints in perfect peace,
My burden cast upon the Lord,
And only care my God to please.

Who stoops to clothe a fading flower
Will every needful blessing give,
And fit the creature of an hour
An endless life with him to live.

My Father knows the things I need,
My Father knows, let that suffice,
I trust him now to clothe and feed
His child who on his care relies.

The cause of my misgiving fear,
Lord, I my unbelief confess;
Author of faith in me appear,
And bid my doubts and terrors cease!

Charles Wesley

UPON THE LORD'S PRAYER

Our Father which in heaven art,
Thy name be always hallowed;
Thy kingdom come, thy will be done;
Thy heavenly path be followed
By us on earth as 'tis with thee,
We humbly pray;
And let our bread us given be,
From day to day.
Forgive our debts as we forgive
Those that to us indebted are:
Into temptation lead us not,
But save us from the wicked snare.
The kingdom's thine, the power too,
We thee adore;
The glory also shall be thine
For evermore.

John Bunyan

THE WISE PERSON
(from Matthew 7)

Whoso therefore these sayings of mine doth hear,
And doth them, to a wise man I'll compare,
The which upon a rock his building founded,
The rain descended and the floods surrounded,
The winds arose, and gave it many a shock,
And it fell not, being founded on a rock.
And ev'ry one that hears these sayings of mine,
And not to do them doth his heart incline,
Unto a foolish man shall be compar'd;
Who his foundation on the sand prepar'd:
The rain descended and the floods were great,
The winds did blow, and vehemently beat
Against that house; and down the building came,
And mighty was the downfall of the same.

John Bunyan

LEARN OF ME
(Take my yoke upon you, and learn of me – Matthew 11.29)

Lord, I fain would learn of Thee
Meekness and humility;
In Thy gentleness of mind
  In Thy lowliness of heart
Rest mine inmost soul shall find,
  Rest that never can depart.

Charles Wesley

THE SEEING EYE
(They seeing see not; and hearing they hear not – Matthew 13.13)

Saviour I still to thee apply,
  Before I read or hear,
Creator of the seeing eye,
  And of the hearing ear:
The understanding heart bestow,
  The wisdom from above

So shall I all thy doctrines know,
And all thy sayings love.

Charles Wesley

I KNOW DE LORD'S LAID HIS HANDS ON ME

Did ever you see de like before?
I know de Lord's laid his hands on me.
King Jesus preachin' to de poor;
I know de Lord's laid his hands on me.

My Lord done jes' what he said;
I know de Lord's laid his hands on me.
He heal de sick an' raise de dead,
I know de Lord's laid his hands on me.

Some seek de Lord an' doan' seek him right;
I know de Lord's laid his hands on me.
Dey fool all day an' pray at night;
I know de Lord's laid his hands on me.

Traditional Black American Spiritual

ESSENTIAL TRUTH

(He that sent me is true – John 7.28
These things saith he that is . . . true, he that hath the key of David –
Revelation 3.7
The Spirit is truth – 1 John 5.6)

Who sent the Son is true;
    True is the Son that came;
True is the Spirit too,
Conferred in Jesus' name:
The Father, Son, and Holy Ghost
    Essential truth we own,
And prostrate with His heavenly host
    Adore the Three in One.

Charles Wesley

THE TRANSFIGURATION
(There appeared unto them Elias with Moses – Mark 9.4)

Who Moses and the prophets hear,
   And Christ the Sum of all receive,
Transfigured shall with Christ appear,
   With him in light and glory live,
Obtain a never-fading crown,
   Enraptured on their Saviour gaze,
For ever by his side sit down,
   And talk with Jesus face to face.

Charles Wesley

THE PRODIGAL SON
(From God's Trombones)

Young man –
Young man –
Your arm's too short to box with God.

But Jesus spake in a parable, and he said:
A certain man had two sons.
Jesus didn't give this man a name,
But his name is God Almighty.
And Jesus didn't call these sons by name,
But ev'ry young man,
Ev'rywhere,
Is one of these two sons.

And the younger son said to his father,
he said: Father, divide up the property,
And give me my portion now.

And the father with tears in his eyes said: Son,
Don't leave your father's house.
But the boy was stubborn in his head,
And haughty in his heart,
And he took his share of his father's goods,
And went into a far-off country.

There comes a time,
There comes a time
When ev'ry young man looks out from his father's house,
Longing for that far-off country.

And the young man journeyed on his way,
And he said to himself as he traveled along:
This sure is an easy road,
Nothing like the rough furrows behind my father's plow.

Young man –
Young man –
Smooth and easy is the road
That leads to hell and destruction.
Down grade all the way,
The further you travel, the faster you go.
No need to trudge and sweat and toil,
Just slip and slide and slip and slide
Till you bang up against hell's iron gate.

And the younger son kept travelling along,
Till at night-time he came to a city.
And the city was bright in the night-time like day,
The streets all crowded with people,
Brass bands and string bands a-playing,
And ev'rywhere the young man turned
There was singing and laughing and dancing.
And he stopped a passer-by and he said:
Tell me what city is this?
And the passer-by laughed and said: Don't you know?
This is Babylon, Babylon,
That great city of Babylon.
Come on, my friend, and go along with me.
And the young man joined the crowd.

Young man –
Young man –
You're never lonesome in Babylon.
You can always join a crowd in Babylon.
Young man –
Young man –
You can never be alone in Babylon,
Alone with your Jesus in Babylon.

You can never find a place, a lonesome place,
A lonesome place to go down on your knees,
And talk with your God, in Babylon.
You're always in a crowd in Babylon.

And the young man went with his new-found friend,
And bought himself some brand new clothes,
And he spent his days in the drinking dens,
Swallowing the fires of hell.
And he spent his nights in the gambling dens,
Throwing dice with the devil for his soul.
And he met up with the women of Babylon.
Oh, the women of Babylon!
Dressed in yellow and purple and scarlet,
Loaded with rings and earrings and bracelets,
Their lips like a honeycomb dripping with honey,
Perfumed and sweet-smelling like a jasmine flower;
And the jasmine smell of the Babylon women
Got in his nostrils and went to his head,
And he wasted his substance in riotous living,
In the evening, in the black and dark of night,
With the sweet-sinning women of Babylon.
And they stripped him of his money,
And they stripped him of his clothes,
And they left him broke and ragged
In the streets of Babylon.

Then the young man joined another crowd –
The beggars and lepers of Babylon.
And he went to feeding swine,
And he was hungrier than the hogs;
He got down on his belly in the mire and mud
And ate the husks with the hogs.
And not a hog was too low to turn up his nose
At the man in the mire of Babylon.

Then the young man came to himself –
He came to himself and said:
In my father's house are many mansions,
Ev'ry servant in his house has bread to eat,
Ev'ry servant in his house has a place to sleep;
I will arise and go to my father.

And his father saw him afar off,
And he ran up the road to meet him.
He put clean clothes upon his back,
And a golden chain around his neck,
He made a feast and killed the fatted calf,
And invited the neighbours in.

Oh-o-oh, sinner,
When you're mingling with the crowd in Babylon –
Drinking the wine of Babylon –
Running with the women of Babylon –
You forget about God, and you laugh at Death.
Today you've got the strength of a bull in your neck
And the strength of a bear in your arms,
But some o' these days, some o' these days,
You'll have a hand-to-hand struggle with bony Death,
And Death is bound to win.

Young man, come away from Babylon,
That hell-border city of Babylon.
Leave the dancing and gambling of Babylon,
The wine and whiskey of Babylon,
The hot-mouthed women of Babylon;
Fall down on your knees,
And say in your heart:
I will arise and go to my Father.

James Weldon Johnson

DIVES AND LAZARUS

As it fell out upon a day
    Rich Dives he made a feast,
And he invited all his friends
    And gentry of the best.

Then Lazarus laid him down and down
    And down at Dives' door:
Some meat, some drink, brother Dives,
    Bestow upon the poor.

Thou art none of my brother, Lazarus,
    That lies begging at my door;
No meat nor drink will I give thee
    Nor bestow upon the poor.

Then Lazarus laid him down and down
    And down at Dives' wall:
Some meat, some drink, brother Dives,
    Or with hunger starve I shall.

Thou art none of my brother, Lazarus,
    That lies begging at my wall;
No meat nor drink will I give thee
    But with hunger starve you shall.

Then Lazarus laid him down and down
    And down at Dives' gate:
Some meat, some drink, brother Dives,
    For Jesus Christ his sake.

Thou art none of my brother, Lazarus,
    That lies begging at my gate;
No meat nor drink will I give thee
    For Jesus Christ his sake.

Then Dives sent out his merry men
    To whip poor Lazarus away;
They had no power to strike a stroke
    But flung their whips away.

Then Dives sent out his hungry dogs
    To bite him as he lay;
They had no power to bite at all
    But licked his sores away.

As it fell out upon a day
    Poor Lazarus sickened and died;
Then came two angels out of heaven
    His soul therein to guide.

Rise up, rise up, brother Lazarus,
    And go along with me;
For you've a place prepared in heaven
    To sit on an angel's knee.

As it fell out upon a day
    Rich Dives sickened and died
Then came two serpents out of hell
    His soul therein to guide.

Rise up, rise up, brother Dives,
    And go with us to see
A dismal place prepared in hell
    From which thou canst not flee.

Then Dives looked up with his eyes
    And saw poor Lazarus blest:
Give me one drop of water, brother Lazarus,
    To quench my flaming thirst.

Oh had I as many years to abide
    As there are blades of grass,
Then there would be an end, but now
    Hell's pains will ne'er be past.

Oh was I now but alive again
    The space of one half hour;
Oh that I had my peace secure;
    Then the devil should have no power.

Anon. (Traditional Ballad)

TWO WENT UP INTO THE TEMPLE
TO PRAY

Two went to pray? O rather say
One went to brag, th' other to pray:

One stands up close and treads on high,
Where th' other dares not send his eye.

One nearer to God's altar trod,
The other to the altar's God.

Richard Crashaw

TO OUR LORD, UPON THE WATER MADE WINE

Thou water turn'st to wine, fair friend of life,
Thy foe, to cross the sweet arts of thy reign,
Distils from thence the tears of wrath and strife,
And so turns wine to water back again.

Richard Crashaw

ON THE MIRACLE OF THE MULTIPLIED LOAVES

See here an easy feast that knows no wound,
    That under hunger's teeth will needs be sound;
A subtle harvest of unbounded bread,
    What would ye more? Here food itself is fed.

Richard Crashaw

THE FIELD OF THE WORLD
(Matthew 13.37–43)

This is the field, the world below,
In which the sowers came to sow,
Jesus the wheat, Satan the tares,
For so the word of truth declares:
And soon the reaping time will come,
And angels shout the harvest home.

Most awful truth! and is it so?
Must all the world that harvest know?
Is every man a wheat or tare?
Then for that harvest O prepare!
For soon the reaping time will come,
And angels shout the harvest home.

To love my sins, – a saint to appear,
To grow with wheat – yet be a tare,
May serve me while I live below,
Where tares and wheat together grow:
But soon the reaping time will come,
And angels shout the harvest home.

But all who truly righteous be
Their Father's kingdom then shall see;
And shine like suns for ever there:
He that hath ears, now let him hear;
For soon the reaping time will come,
And angels shout the harvest home.

Anon.

JESUS MET THE WOMAN

Jesus met the woman at the well,
And he told her ev'rything she'd ever done.

He said: 'Woman, Woman, where is your husband?
I know ev'ry thing you've ever done.'

She said: 'Jesus, Jesus, ain't got no husband
And You don't know ev'rything I've ever done.'

He said: 'Woman, woman, you've got five husbands
And the one you have now, he's not your own.'

She said: 'This man, this man, he must be a prophet,
He done told me ev'rything I've ever done.'

Traditional Black American Spiritual

I HEARD THE VOICE OF JESUS SAY

I heard the voice of Jesus say
'Come unto Me and rest;
Lay down, thou weary one, lay down
Thy head upon My breast':

I came to Jesus as I was,
Weary, and worn, and sad
I found in him a resting-place,
And he has made me glad.

I heard the voice of Jesus say,
'Behold, I freely give
The living water; thirsty one,
Stoop down, and drink, and live':
I came to Jesus and I drank
Of that life-giving stream;
My thirst was quenched, my soul revived,
And now I live in him.

I heard the voice of Jesus say,
'I am this dark world's light;
Look unto Me, thy morn shall rise,
And all thy day be bright':
I looked to Jesus, and I found
In Him my star, my sun
And in that light of life I'll walk
Till travelling days are done.

Horatius Bonar (1808–89)

STAN' BY ME!
(Mark 4.41)

When de storm of life is ragin'
When de world is tossin' me
Like a ship upon de sea,
Thou who rulest wind an' water,
Oh, stan' by me.

In de midst of tribulation
When de hosts of hell assail me,
An' my strength begins to fail me,
Thou who never lost a battle,
Oh, stan' by me.

In de midst of faults and failures,
When I do de bes' I can,
An' my friends misunderstan'
Thou who knowest all about me,
Oh, stan' by me.

In de midst of persecution,
When my foes in battle array,
Undertake to stop my way,
Thou who stood by Paul an' Silas,
Oh, stan' by me.

When I'm growin' old an' feeble,
When my life becomes a burden,
An' I'm nearin' chilly Jordan,
Oh, thou Lily of de Valley,
Stan' by me, stan' by me!

Traditional Black American Spiritual

THERE IS NO LOVE ON EARTH
AS GREAT AS THINE
(John 17.24)

There is no love on earth as great as Thine,
    Nor height, nor depth that love can separate;
And for Thy ransomed ones, eternal praise is their sweet fate.

There is no love on earth can keep me here,
    Take me to be with Thee, since I am Thine,
And Thou hast all my needs fulfilled and met; Thou mighty Vine.

There was no love on earth full great enough,
    But heaven alone could that great love supply;
And so in love, before the stars were made, the Lamb chose me.

Linette Martin

THE WORD

'*Forsaking all*' – You mean
head over heels, for good,
for ever, call of the depths
of the All – the heart of one
who creates all, at every
moment, newly – for
you do so – and
to me, far fallen in the
ashheaps of my
false-making, burnt-out self and in the
hosed-down rubble of what my furores
gutted, or sooted all
around me – you implore
me to so fall
in Love, and fall anew in
ever-new depths of skywashed Love till every
capillary of your universe
throbs with your rivering fire?

'*Forsaking all*' – Your voice
never falters, and yet,
unsealing day out of a
darkness none ever knew
in full but you,
you spoke that word, closing on it forever:
'Why hast Thou forsaken . . .?'

This measure of your being all-out, and
meaning it, made you
put it all on the line
we, humanly, wanted to draw – at
having you teacher only, or
popular spokesman only, or
doctor or simply a source of sanity
for us, distracted, or only
the one who could wholeheartedly
rejoice with us, and know
our tears, our flickering time, and
stand with us.

But to make it head over heels
yielding, all the way,
you had to die for us.
The line we drew, you crossed,
and cross out, wholly forget,
at the faintest stirring of what
you know is love, is One
whose name has been, and is
and will be, the
I AM.

Margaret Avison (b. 1918)

'NEITHER DURST ANY MAN FROM THAT DAY ASK HIM ANY MORE QUESTIONS'
(Matthew 22)

Midst all the dark and knotty snares
Black wit or malice can or dares
Thy glorious wisdom breaks the nets
And treads with uncontrolled steps.
Thy quelled foes are not only now
Thy triumphs, but Thy trophies too;
They both at once Thy conquests be
And Thy conquest's memory.
Stony amazement makes them stand
Waiting on Thy victorious hand,
Like statues fixed to the fame
Of Thy renown and their own shame
As if they only meant to breathe
To be the life of their own death.
'Twas time to hold their peace when they
Had ne'er another word to say;
Yet is their silence unto Thee
The full sound of Thy victory.
Their silence speaks aloud and is
Thy well-pronounced panegyris.
While they speak nothing, they speak all
Their share in Thy memorial.

While they speak nothing, they proclaim
Thee with the shrillest trump of fame
    To hold their peace is all the ways
    These wretches have to speak Thy praise.

Richard Crashaw

panegyris: a general assembly gathered to praise or eulogize

RIDE ON, KING JESUS!

I was but young when I began,
No man can-a hinder me,
But now my race is almost done,
No man can-a hinder me.

Ride on, King Jesus,
No man can-a hinder me.
Ride on, King Jesus,
No man can-a hinder me.

King Jesus rides a milk-white horse,
No man can-a hinder me.
The river of Jordan he did cross,
No man can-a hinder me.

Traditional Black American Spiritual

THE UPPER ROOM

In that sad memorable night,
    When Jesus was for us betrayed,
He left his death-recording rite,
    He took, and blessed, and brake the bread,
And gave his own their last bequest,
And thus his love's intent exprest;

Take, eat, this is my body, given
    To purchase life and peace for you,
Pardon and holiness and heaven;
    Do this my dying love to show,
Accept your precious legacy,
And thus, my friends, remember me.

He took into his hands the cup,
    To crown the sacramental feast,
And full of kind concern looked up,
    And gave what he to them had blest;
And drink ye all of this, he said,
In solemn memory of the Dead.

This is my blood which seals the new
    Eternal covenant of my grace,
My blood so freely shed for you,
    For you and all the sinful race;
My blood that speaks your sins forgiven,
And justifies your claim to heaven.

The grace which I to all bequeath
    In this divine memorial take,
And, mindful of your Saviour's death,
    Do this, my followers, for my sake,
Whose dying love hath left behind
Eternal life for all mankind.

Charles Wesley

IN THE SAME NIGHT IN WHICH
HE WAS BETRAYED

In the same night in which he was betrayed,
    The supper ended, and the dark come down,
There in that lonely garden Jesus prayed,
    Beyond the lamplight of the sleeping town:
        Above the trees the Paschal moon is high,
        The olive branches black against the sky.

What agony of spirit bowed his head
    Lies far beyond our human heart to frame;
Yet 'Not my will but yours' at last he said,
      As lights and torches through the garden came:
          So Judas ends what love of self began,
          And with a kiss betrays the Son of Man.

The hour is come: the power of darkness reigns.
    See, like a lamb, the Lord is led away.
Of twelve disciples only one remains
    To wait the dawning of the final day:
          Alone before his captors Jesus stands,
          While in the courtyard Peter warms his hands.

★ ★ ★

Turn, Lord and look: for many a cock has crowed;
    We too betray, forsake you, or deny.
For us, like Peter, bitter tears have flowed,
    Lost in the dark, no language but a cry;
          A cry of weakness, failure and despair:
          Lord, in your mercy, stoop to hear our prayer.

Timothy Dudley-Smith

THE LOOK

The Saviour looked on Peter. Ay, no word,
No gesture of reproach: the heavens serene,
Though heavy with armed justice, did not lean
Their thunders that way: the forsaken Lord
Looked only on the traitor. None record
What that look was, none guess; for those who have seen
Wronged lovers loving through a death-pang keen,
Or pale-cheeked martyrs smiling to a sword,
Have missed Jehovah at the judgment-call.
And Peter, from the height of blasphemy –
'I never knew this man' – did quail and fall,
As knowing straight *that* God, and turnèd free,
And went out speechless from the face of all,
And filled the silence, weeping bitterly.

Elizabeth Barrett Browning (1806–61)

THE MEANING OF THE LOOK

I think that look of Christ might seem to say,
'Thou Peter! art thou, then, a common stone
Which I at last must break my heart upon,
For all God's charge to His high angels may
Guard my foot better? Did I yesterday
Wash *thy* feet, my beloved, that they should run
Quick to deny me 'neath the morning sun?
And do thy kisses, like the rest, betray?
The cock crows coldly. Go, and manifest
A late contrition, but no bootless fear;
For, when thy final need is dreariest,
Thou shalt not be denied, as I am here:
My voice to God and angels shall attest,
"Because I *know* this man, let him be clear." '

Elizabeth Barrett Browning

DE JEWS, DEY TOOK OUR SAVIOUR

De Jews, dey took our Saviour an' dey buried him in sepulchre,
Dey place' de watchman 'side his grave
For ter see him when he rose,
I believe dey said, 'ter see him when he rose.'

Go low down in de valley,
Go low down in de valley, good Lord,
For ter easy mah trouble in min(d),
I believe dey said, 'ter easy mah trouble in min(d).'

A yonder comes ole Sat'n wid a black Bible under his arm,
He said unto ole Moses:
'Now one half o' dem people is mine,'
I believe he said, 'One half o' dem people is mine.'

Traditional Black American Spiritual

MARY MOTHER, COME AND SEE

'Mary mother, come and see:
  Thy Son is nailèd on a tree.

'His body is wrappèd all in woe,
Hand and foot; he may not go;
Thy son, lady, that thou lovest so,
  Naked is nailed upon a tree.

'The blessèd body that thou hast borne
To save mankind, that was forelorn,
His body, lady, is all too-torn,
  His head with thorns, as ye may see.'

When Johan this tale began to tell,
Mary would not longer dwell
Till she came to that hill
  There she might her own Son see.

'My sweet Son, thou art my dear;
Why have men hung thee here?
Thy head is closèd with a briar;
  Why have men so done to thee?'

'Johan, this woman I thee betake;
Keep this woman for my sake;
On the rood I hang for mannès sake,
  For sinful man, as thou may see.

'This game and love me must ply
For sinful souls that are to die;
There is no man that goeth by the way
  That on my pains will look and see.

'Father, my soul I thee betake;
My body death for mannès sake;
To hell I go withoutèn wake,
  Mannès soul to make free.'

Pray we all to that blessèd Son
That he us help when we not mon,
And bring us to bliss that is abone.
Amen, amen, amen, for charity.

Anon. (fifteenth–sixteenth century)

I thee betake: to thee I commit; **we not mon**: we may not (help ourselves); **abone**: above

OH, MARY, DOAN' YER WEEP

Oh, Mary, doan' yer weep, doan' yer moan,
Oh, Mary, doan' yer weep, doan' yer moan,
Pharaoh's army got drownded,
Oh, Mary, doan' yer weep.

Ain't been to heav'n, but I' been tol':
Streets is pearl an' de houses is gol',
Pharaoh's army got drownded,
Oh, Mary, doan' yer weep.

Doan' know what my mother stays here fer,
Dis worl' ain' very good to her,
Pharaoh's army got drownded,
Oh, Mary, doan' yer weep.

Jesus done jes' as he said,
He heal de sick an' he rais' a dead,
Pharaoh's army got drownded,
Oh, Mary, doan' yer weep.

Traditional Black American Spiritual

WEEPIN' MARY

Weepin' Mary,
Weep no more,
Weepin' Mary,
Weep no more:

They nail'd him to the cross,
With a spear they pierced his side.
While the blood trickled down
He bow'd
His head.

Weepin' Mary,
Weep no more,
Weepin' Mary,
Weep no more:

He bow'd his head to die no more,
He rose from the dead;
He's a comin' again on the Judgment Day,
on the
Judgment Day.

Doubtin' Thomas,
Doubt no more
Doubtin' Thomas,
Doubt no more.

Traditional Black American Spiritual

INDIFFERENCE

When Jesus came to Golgotha they hanged him on a tree,
They drave great nails through hands and feet, and made a Calvary;
They crowned him with a crown of thorns, red were his wounds
    and deep,
For those were crude and cruel days, and human flesh was cheap.

When Jesus came to Birmingham, they simply passed him by,
They never hurt a hair of him, they only let him die;
For men had grown more tender, and they would not give him pain.
They only just passed down the street, and left him in the rain.

Still Jesus cried, 'Forgive them, for they know not what they do',
And still it rained the wintry rain that drenched him through
　　and through;
The crowds went home and left the streets without a soul to see,
And Jesus crouched against a wall and cried for Calvary.
G. A. Studdert Kennedy (1883–1929)

SING A-HO THAT I HAD THE WINGS OF A DOVE

Sing a-ho that I had the wings of a dove;
I'd fly away an' be at rest.

Virgin Mary had one Son,
I'd fly away an' be at rest.
The Jews an' the Romans had Him hung,
I'd fly away an' be at rest.

Zion's daughters wept an' mourn'd
I'd fly away an' be at rest.
When their dyin' Saviour groan'd,
I'd fly away an' be at rest.

Sinner man, see what a shame,
I'd fly away an' be at rest.
To trample down your Saviour's name,
I'd fly away an' be at rest.

Sing a-ho that I had the wings of a dove;
I'd fly away an' be at rest.
Traditional Black American Spiritual

A DREAM OF THE CROSS
(Dream of the Rood)

Lo! I will tell   the dearest of dreams
That I dreamed in the midnight   when mortal men
Were sunk in slumber.   Me-seemed I saw
A wondrous Tree   towering in air,
Most shining of crosses   compassed with light.
Brightly that beacon   was gilded with gold;
Jewels adorned it   fair at the foot,
Five on the shoulder-beam,   blazing in splendour.
Through all creation   the angels of God
Beheld it shining –   no cross of shame!
Holy spirits   gazed on its gleaming,
Men upon earth   and all this great creation.
        Wondrous that Tree,   that Token of triumph,
And I a transgressor   soiled with my sins!
I gazed on the Rood   arrayed in glory,
Shining in beauty   and gilded with gold,
The Cross of the Saviour   beset with gems.
But through the gold-work   outgleamed a token
Of the ancient evil   of sinful men
Where the Rood on its right side   once sweat blood.
Saddened and rueful,   smitten with terror
At the wondrous Vision,   I saw the Cross
Swiftly varying   vesture and hue,
Now wet and stained   with the Blood outwelling,
Now fairly jewelled   with gold and gems.
        Then, as I lay there,   long I gazed
In rue and sadness   on my Saviour's Tree,
Till I heard in dream   how the Cross addressed me,
Of all woods worthiest,   speaking these words:
        'Long years ago   (well yet I remember)
They hewed me down   on the edge of the holt,
Severed my trunk;   strong foemen took me,
For a spectacle wrought me,   a gallows for rogues.
High on their shoulders   they bore me to a hilltop,
Fastened me firmly,   an army of foes!
        'Then I saw the King   of all mankind
In brave mood hasting   to mount upon me.
Refuse I dared not,   nor bow nor break,
Though I felt earth's confines   shudder in fear;

All foes I might fell,   yet still I stood fast.
        'Then the young Warrior,   God, the All-Wielder,
Put off His raiment,   steadfast and strong;
With lordly mood   in the sight of many
He mounted the Cross   to redeem mankind.
When the Hero clasped me   I trembled in terror,
But I dared not bow me   nor bend to earth;
I must needs stand fast.   Upraised as the Rood
I held the High King,   the Lord of heaven.
I dared not bow!   With black nails driven
Those sinners pierced me;   the prints are clear,
The open wounds.   I dared injure none.
They mocked us both.   I was wet with blood
From the Hero's side   when He sent forth His spirit.
        'Many a bale   I bore on that hill-side
Seeing the Lord   in agony outstretched.
Black darkness covered   with clouds God's body,
That radiant splendour.   Shadow went forth
Wan under heaven;   all creation wept
Bewailing the King's death.   Christ was on the Cross.
        'Then many came quickly,   faring from far,
Hurrying to the Prince.   I beheld it all.
Sorely smitten with sorrow   in meekness I bowed
To the hands of men.   From His heavy and bitter pain
They lifted Almighty God.   Those warriors left me
Standing bespattered with blood;   I was wounded with spears.
Limb-weary they laid Him down;   they stood at His head,
Looked on the Lord of heaven   as He lay there at rest
From His bitter ordeal all forspent.   In sight of His slayers
They made Him a sepulchre   carved from the shining stone;
Therein laid the Lord of triumph.   At evening tide
Sadly they sang their dirges   and wearily turned away
From their lordly Prince;   there He lay all still and alone.
        'There at our station   a long time we stood
Sorrowfully weeping   after the wailing of men
Had died away.   The corpse grew cold,
The fair life-dwelling.   Down to earth
Men hacked and felled us,   a grievous fate!
They dug a pit   and buried us deep.
But there God's friends   and followers found me
And graced me with treasure   of silver and gold.
        'Now may you learn,   O man beloved,

The bitter sorrows   that I have borne,
The work of caitiffs.   But the time is come
That men upon earth   and through all creation
Show me honour   and bow to this sign.
On me a while   God's Son once suffered;
Now I tower under heaven   in glory attired
With healing for all   that hold me in awe.
Of old I was once   the most woeful of tortures,
Most hateful to all men,   till I opened for them
The true Way of life.   Lo! the Lord of glory,
The Warden of heaven,   above all wood
Has glorified me   as Almighty God
Has honoured His Mother,   even Mary herself,
Over all womankind   in the eyes of men.
     'Now I give you bidding,   O man beloved,
Reveal this Vision   to the sons of men,
And clearly tell   of the Tree of glory
Whereon God suffered   for man's many sins
And the evil that Adam   once wrought of old.
     'Death He suffered,   but our Saviour rose
By virtue of His great might   as a help to men.
He ascended to heaven.   But hither again
He shall come unto earth   to seek mankind,
The Lord Himself   on the Day of Doom,
Almighty God   with His angel hosts.
And then will He judge,   Who has power of judgment,
To each man according   as here on earth
In this fleeting life   he shall win reward.
     'Nor there may any   be free from fear
Hearing the words   which the Wielder shall utter.
He shall ask before many: Where is the man
Who would taste bitter death   as He did on the Tree?
And all shall be fearful   and few shall know
What to say unto Christ.   But none at His Coming
Shall need to fear   if he bears in his breast
This best of symbols;   and every soul
From the ways of earth   through the Cross shall come
To heavenly glory,   who would dwell with God.'
     Then with ardent spirit   and earnest zeal,
Companionless, lonely,   I prayed to the Cross.
My soul was fain of death.   I had endured
Many an hour of longing.   It is my life's hope

That I may turn   to this Token of triumph,
I above all men,   and revere it well.
      This is my heart's desire,   and all my hope
Waits on the Cross.   In this world now
I have few powerful friends;   they have fared hence
Away from these earthly gauds   seeking the King of glory,
Dwelling now with the High Father   in heaven above,
Abiding in rapture.   Each day I dream
Of the hour when the Cross of my Lord,   whereof here on earth
I once had vision,   from this fleeting life may fetch me
And bring me where is great gladness   and heavenly bliss,
Where the people of God   are planted and stablished for ever
In joy everlasting.   There may it lodge me
Where I may abide in glory   knowing bliss with the saints.
      May the Lord befriend me   who on earth of old
Once suffered on the Cross   for the sins of men.
He redeemed us, endowed us with life   and a heavenly home.
Therein was hope renewed   with blessing and bliss
For those who endured the burning.   In that great deed
God's Son was triumphant,   possessing power and strength!
Almighty, Sole-Ruling   He came to the kingdom of God
Bringing a host of souls   to angelic bliss,
To join the saints   who abode in the splendour of glory,
When the Lord, Almighty God,   came again to His throne.
Trans. Charles W. Kennedy (Early English)

caitiffs: evil-doers

THE CRUCIFIXION
(He never said a mumbelin' word)

Oh, wasn't that a pity an' a shame?
An' he never said a mumbelin' word.
They carried him to Pilate's bar,
An' he never said a mumbelin' word;
Not a word.

They led him up to Calv'ry's hill,
An' he never said a mumbelin' word,
They nail'd him to the tree,
An' he never said a mumbelin' word,
Not a word.

They pierced him in the side,
An' he never said a mumbelin' word,
He bow'd his head an' died.
An' he never said a mumbelin' word,
Not a word.

Traditional Black American Spiritual

CRUCIFIXION HYMN

Now is the noon of sorrow's night,
High in his patience as their spite.
Lo, the faint Lamb with weary limb
Bears that huge tree which must bear Him.
That fatal plant, so great of fame
For fruit of sorrow and of shame,
Shall swell with both for Him and mix
All woes into one crucifix.
Is tortured thirst itself too sweet a cup?
Gall and more bitter mocks shall make it up.
Are nails blunt pens of superficial smart?
Contempt and scorn can send sure sounds
     to search the inmost Heart.

Richard Crashaw

ON OUR CRUCIFIED LORD
NAKED AND BLOODY

They have left Thee naked, Lord, O that they had;
This garment too I would they had denied.
Thee with Thyself they have too richly clad,
Opening the purpose wardrobe of Thy side.
  O never could be found garments too good
For Thee to wear, but these of Thine own blood.

Richard Crashaw

THE WINDS

There is a tree grows upside down,
  Its roots are in the sky;
Its lower branches reach the earth
  When amorous winds are nigh.

On one lone bough there strakly hangs
  A Man just crucified,
And all the other branches beat
  The choice fruits of the Bride.

When Pleasure's wind goes frisking past,
  Unhallowed by a prayer
It swirls dead leaves from earth-born trees,
  Old growths of pride and care.

The gracious fruits are hidden by
  These leaves of human stain;
The Crucified beneath His load
  Shudders, as if in pain.

But swift springs down a credal wind,
  It thrills through all the boughs,
The dead leaves scatter and are lost;
  The Christ renews His vows.

His hands direct the Spirit's wind
  Branch after branch to shake;
The bride's fruit drops, and at the touch
  Elected hearts awake.

Jack Clemo (1916–74)

A QUIET ROAR

one

he lays his left hand along the beam
hand that moulded clay into fluttering birds
hand that cupped wild flowers to learn their peace
hand that stroked the bee's soft back and touched death's sting

two

he stretches his right hand across the grain
hand that blessed a dead corpse quick
hand that smeared blind spittle into sight
hand that burgeoned bread, smoothed down the rumpled sea

three

he stands laborious
sagging, split,
homo erectus, poor bare forked thing
hung on nails like a picture

he is not beautiful
blood sweats from him in rain

far off where we are lost, desert dry
thunder begins its quiet roar
the first drops startle us alive
the cloud no bigger
than a man's hand

Veronica Zundel

THE SERVANT KING

From heaven you came, helpless babe,
entered our world, your glory veiled;
not to be served but to serve,
and give your life that we might live.

This is our God, the Servant King,
he calls us now to follow him,
to bring our lives as a daily offering
of worship to the Servant King.

There in the garden of tears,
my heavy load he chose to bear;
his heart with sorrow was torn,
'Yet not my will but yours,' he said.

Come see his hands and his feet,
the scars that speak of sacrifice,
hands that flung stars into space
to cruel nails surrendered.

So let us learn how to serve,
and in our lives enthrone him;
each other's needs to prefer,
for it is Christ we're serving.

Graham Kendrick (b. 1950)

MARY MAGDALEN'S COMPLAINT AT THE DEATH OF CHRIST

Silly stars must needs leave shining
  When the sun is shadowèd,
Borrowed streams refrain their running
  When head springs are hinderèd:
One that lives by other's breath,
Dieth also by his death.

O true life! Sith Thou hast left me
  Mortal life is tedious;
Death it is to live without Thee,
  Death of all most odious;
Turn again or take me to Thee,
Let me die or live Thou in me!

Where the truth once was and is not,
  Shadows are but vanity;
Shewing want, that help they cannot,
  Signs, not salves, of misery.
Painted meat no longer feeds,
Dying life each death exceeds.

With my love my life was nestled
  In the sum of happiness;
From my love my life is wrested
  To a world of heaviness.
O let love my life remove
Sith I live not where I love!

O my soul! What did unloose thee
  From thy sweet captivity?
God, not I, did still possess thee,
  His, not mine, thy liberty.
O too happy thrall thou wert,
When thy prison was His heart.

Spiteful spear that break'st this prison,
  Seat of all felicity,
Working thus with double treason
  Love's and life's delivery:
Though my life thou drav'st away,
Maugre thee my love shall stay.

Robert Southwell (?1561–95)

WERE YOU THERE?

Were you there when they crucified my Lord?
Oh! Sometimes it causes me to tremble, brothers, tremble
Were you there when they crucified my Lord?

Were you there when they laid him in the tomb?
Oh! Sometimes it causes me to tremble, brothers, tremble
Were you there when they laid him in the tomb?

Traditional Black American Spiritual

ROSE GARDEN

We buried you in rose petals –
  no time for normal grief,
so sudden your taking
  by pitiless hands.

The scent-heavy soft petals
  covered hideous wounds.
Even in death your dignity stopped you hanging
  forlorn to become bleached bones.

When we returned at the breaking
  of next day to confine you properly
one of us remarked at the
  pale beauty of the lighting sky.

Then it was that we saw
  what seemed like many birds
wheeling and diving and dancing –
  dark hectic spots in the rose splendour.

The pattern of glory held us breathless
  in its weaving, fluent spell.
Oh but then the sky began falling,
  the spots became dark snow upon us.

Turning all ways we realized from touch
  and wonder that heaven was shedding petals –
these soft rose leaves were those
  birds, your dancers in the sky.

We looked at each other, awe
  in our still upturned faces,
then we rushed to your tomb in the cold rocks
  to see our last petals still whirling up to heaven.

Your tomb was vacant – with even
  the dust scoured out of the cave:
no mutilated, lovely body, cursed
  by death; not even one petal left lying.

So, then a sign. Our gift of petals had multiplied
  into skyborne myriads – more numerous than
the fading stars seen poured across
  the night so little time before.

We turned from peering into absence,
  glancing back suddenly to a winter garden
soft underfoot, deep with our petals,
  stirred by a sudden fragrant wind

in which you walked toward us.

Colin Duriez

EASTER DAY

Rise, Heir of fresh eternity
  From Thy virgin tomb
Rise, Mighty Man of Wonders, and Thy world with Thee;
  Thy tomb, the universal east,
  Nature's new womb,
Thy tomb, fair immortality's perfumed nest.

Of all the glories making noon gay
  This is the morn.
This rock buds forth the fountains of the streams of day.
  In joy's white annals live this hour
  When Life was torn;
No cloud scowl on His radiant lids, no tempest lower.

Life, by this Light's nativity
  All creatures have.
Death only by this day's just doom is forced to die.
  Nor is death forced, for he may lie
  Throned in Thy grave;
Death will on this condition be content to die.

Richard Crashaw

WHEN MARY THRO'
THE GARDEN WENT

When Mary thro' the garden went
  There was no sound of any bird,
And yet, because the night was spent,
  The little grasses lightly stirred,
  The flowers awoke, the lilies heard.

When Mary thro' the garden went,
  The dew lay still on flower and grass,
The waving palms about her sent
  Their fragrance out as she did pass,
  No light upon the branches was.

When Mary thro' the garden went,
   Her eyes, for weeping long, were dim,
The grass beneath her footsteps bent,
   The solemn lilies, white and slim,
   These also stood and wept for him.

When Mary thro' the garden went,
   She sought, within the garden ground,
One for whom her heart was rent,
   One who for her sake was bound,
   One who sought and she was found.

Mary Coleridge (1861–1907)

THERE WAS NO

There was no grave grave enough
to ground me
to mound me
I broke the balm then slit the shroud
wound round me
that bound me

There was no death dead enough
to dull me
to cull me
I snapped the snake and waned his war
to lull me
to null me

There was no cross cross enough
to nil me
to still me
I hung as gold that bled, and bloomed
A rose that rose and prised the tomb
away from Satan's wilful doom
There was no cross, death, grave
or room
to hold me.

Stewart Henderson

[THE STRANGER]
(Luke 24.17–27, 30–32)

You, stranger, are the only one for whom
Events of recent days remain unknown:
How we expected Jesus on the throne
Of David – but he won a cross and tomb.
Near blinded by impenetrable gloom,
All messianic expectations flown,
We heard grief's obsolete, but were not shown:
For strange reports we cannot yet make room.
    Expounding all the Scriptures, Moses first,
    Their restless minds the stranger sharply turned
    To sufferings of Messiah as the Cursed;
    And all the while their hearts within them burned.
With broken hands the stranger broke the bread:
Their opened eyes saw him who had been dead.

D. A. Carson (b. 1946)

HE EXPOUNDED UNTO THEM IN ALL THE SCRIPTURES THE THINGS CONCERNING HIMSELF
(Luke 24.27)

The Scriptures all with Christ are filled,
    With Jesus, and His will to save,
His birth and death are there revealed,
    His rise and triumph o'er the grave,
His kingdom come in gracious power,
His reign when time shall be no more.

Jesus, divine Interpreter,
    To me Thine oracles unseal,
Then shall I find and taste Thee there,
    Thy truth, and power, and mercy feel,
And nothing know, and nothing see
In all the book of God but Thee.

To me that Spirit of wisdom give
　　Who doth in all Thy members breathe,
Thy sinless life I then shall live,
　　And daily die Thy blessed death,
Fixed in my heart Thy kingdom own,
And rise to Thine eternal throne.

Charles Wesley

SEVEN STANZAS AT EASTER

Make no mistake: if He rose at all
it was as His body;
if the cells' dissolution did not reverse, the molecules
　　reknit, the amino acids rekindle,
the Church will fall.

It was not as the flowers,
each soft Spring recurrent;
it was not as His Spirit in the mouths and fuddled
　　eyes of the eleven apostles;
it was as His flesh: ours.

The same hinged thumbs and toes,
the same valved heart
that – pierced – died, withered, paused, and then
　　regathered out of enduring Might
new strength to enclose.

Let us not mock God with metaphor,
analogy, sidestepping, transcendence;
making of the event a parable, a sign painted in the
　　faded credulity of earlier ages:
let us walk through the door.

The stone is rolled back, not papier-mâché,
not a stone in a story,
but the vast rock of materiality that in the slow
　　grinding of time will eclipse for each of us
the wide light of day.

And if we will have an angel at the tomb,
make it a real angel,
weighty with Max Planck's quanta, vivid with hair,
    opaque in the dawn light, robed in real linen
spun on a definite loom.

Let us not seek to make it less monstrous,
for our own convenience, our own sense of beauty,
lest, awakened in one unthinkable hour, we are
    embarrassed by the miracle,
and crushed by remonstrance.

John Updike (b. 1932)

EASTER

A woman with shoulders bowed only since Friday
steps deep into death's lair.
Stupified by guilt or sorrow or not caring,
the town had been silent as she passed.
Behind the hedges insensible cyclamen
and violets drink life from the dawn,
giving their moisture back to the sky.
They too should have perished with Him,
blasted to their very root hairs
tenacious in the ground. Gather
some for Him and with the aloes
make an ointment for His bloodied brow.

    O joy! Her bitter myrrh
    had become obsolete at daybreak.
    Through ground and rock,
    sky, sea, and stars,
    He bursts His putrid casing
    and confronts the universe!

She folds the linen, taking it home
to wash from it the stench of death,
joyfully laying it out in the forever sunshine.

Carolyn Keefe

THE DUMBFOUNDING

When you walked here,
took skin, muscle, hair,
eyes, larynx, we
withheld all honour: 'His house is clay,
how can he tell us of his far country?'

Your not familiar pace
in flesh, across the waves,
woke only our distrust.
Twice-torn we cried, 'A ghost'
and only on our planks counted you fast.

Dust wet with your spittle
cleared mortal trouble.
We called you a blasphemer,
a devil-tamer.

The evening you spoke of going away
we could not stay.
All legions massed. You had to wash, and rise,
alone, and face
out of the light, for us.

You died.
We said,
'The worst is true, our bliss
has come to this.'

When you were seen by men
in holy flesh again
we hoped so despairingly for such report
we closed their windpipes for it.

Now you have sought
and seek, in all our ways, all thoughts,
streets, musics – and we make of these a din
trying to lock you out, or in,
to be intent. And dying.

Yet you are
constant and sure,
the all-lovely, all-men's-way
to that far country.

Winning one, you again
all ways would begin
life: to make new
flesh, to empower
the weak in nature
to restore
or stay the sufferer;

lead through the garden to
trash, rubble, hill,
where, the outcast's outcast, you
sound dark's uttermost, strangely light-brimming,
  until
time be full.

Margaret Avison

'. . . FOR THEY SHALL SEE GOD'

Christ risen was rarely recognized by sight.
They had to get beyond the way He looked.
Evidence stronger than His voice and face and footstep
waited to grow in them, to guide their groping
out of despair, their stretching toward belief.

We are as blind as they
until the open of our deeper eyes
shows us the hands that bless and break
our bread. Until we finger
wounds that tell our healing, or witness a miracle
of fish, dawn-caught after our long night
of empty nets. Handling His Word,
we feel His flesh, His bones, and hear
His voice saying our early-morning name.

Luci Shaw

THE SINGING CHRIST

Their mighty song burns heavenward
  And glory shines in sound;
The herald angels praise the Lord
  In shouts that shake the ground.
Sing, O sons of heaven's joy,
  The wonder of his ways;
The birth-cry of an infant boy
  Perfects his Father's praise.

Sing, O Jesus, Mary's son,
  The pilgrim psalms appointed:
How great the works the Lord has done!
  How blessèd his Anointed!
Sing in Nazareth, young man,
  The songs of jubilee;
Today fulfill redemption's plan,
  Proclaim the captive free!

Sing, O Saviour, lift the cup,
  'Jehovah is my song!'
The sacrifice is offered up
  Before the shouting throng.
'I come to do thy will, my God,
  My body is prepared
To drink the cup and bear the rod
  That sinners should be spared.'

Sing, O Christ, up Zion's brow
  From Kidron's rocky bed;
The pilgrim songs are silent now
  And all thy friends have fled.
Sing in agony, my King,
  The God-forsaken Lord:
Count thy bones in suffering
  While malice mocks thy word.

Sing, ascending King of kings;
  Lift up your heads, ye gates;
The King of Glory triumph sings,
  The Lord that heaven awaits.

Sing, O Son of God's right hand,
　　Our Prophet, Priest, and King;
The saints that on Mount Zion stand
　　With tongues once dumb now sing.

Sing, Lord Christ, among the choir
　　In robes with blood made white,
And satisfy thy heart's desire
　　To lead the sons of light.
O Chief Musician, Lord of praise,
　　From thee our song is found;
Ancient of everlasting days
　　To thee the trumpets sound.

Rejoicing Saviour, sing today
　　Within our upper room;
Among thy brethren lift the lay
　　Of triumph from the tomb.
Sing now, O Lamb, that we may sing
　　The glory of thy shame,
The paean of thy suffering,
　　To sanctify thy Name!

Edmund P. Clowney (b. 1919)

ON WEEPING
(And they all wept sore – Acts 20.37)

Jesus wept! And never chid
　　Tears of social tenderness;
Saints are not by Him forbid
　　Thus their frailty to confess,
Thus by passion pure to prove
Saints are men of grief and love.

Charles Wesley

BOLD IN OUR ALMIGHTY LORD
(Acts 14.3)

Bold in our Almighty Lord,
While thee we testify,
Present to confirm the word
We on thyself rely;
Thou thy confessors confess,
The truth in sinners' hearts reveal,
Welcome news of saving grace
By thy own Spirit seal.

More than outward wonder show
On those that humbly hear,
Let their souls the witness know,
The indwelling Comforter;
Let their lives resemble thine,
And preach the kingdom from above,
Holy joy and peace divine,
And pure unbounded love.

Thus thy testimony give
To all who speak for thee,
Thus let thousands turn and live
In faith's sincerity;
Through our ministerial hands
Ten thousand more with grace supply,
Power to practise thy commands,
And live for God and die.

Charles Wesley

THE
LETTERS
(Romans to Jude)

The word of faith unto me pardon brings,
Shows me the ground and reason whence it springs:
To wit, free grace, which moved God to give
His Son to die and bleed, that I might live;
This word doth also loudly preach to me,
Though I a miserable sinner be,
Yet in this Son of God I stand complete,
Whose righteousness is without all deceit;
'Tis that which God himself delighteth in,
And that by which all his have savèd been.

John Bunyan (1628–88)

THE JOINING
(After reading Charles Williams and Romans 6)

After the hours of restless
struggling through the waves
of fears, wounded, stroking against
gravity, treading water, stroking,
I choose to let go, to float
numbed, to trust myself to the words
sung across the lake: *Lay down
your life*, to trust my body to
the drifting wood – in weariness my bed,
my frame, the crux of all matters,
to which he was joined by force
but willingly, laid on it to be
what I have been
to gain my pain
(himself to drown in it).

               Thus
am I buoyed, and resting there
cruciform, new knowledge laps me
like a wave: *I* am the cross –
coarse grained and pocked with holes
of nails – to which he joins himself
(already joined to his deep baptism)
that he may join me to his strong escape,
his rising from the darkness of
the icy lake.

Luci Shaw

TO HEAVEN
(Romans 7.24)

Good and great God, can I not think of thee
But it must straight my melancholy be?
Is it interpreted in me disease
That, laden with my sins, I seek for ease?
Oh be thou witness, that the reins dost know
And hearts of all, if I be sad for show,

And judge me after; if I dare pretend
To ought but grace or aim at other end.
As thou art all, so be thou all to me,
First, midst, and last, converted one, and three;
My faith, my hope, my love; and in this state
My judge, my witness, and my advocate.
Where have I been this while exil'd from thee?
And whither rap'd, now thou but stoop'st to me?
Dwell, dwell here still. O, being everywhere,
How can I doubt to find thee ever here?
I know my state, both full of shame and scorn,
Conceiv'd in sin, and unto labour borne,
Standing with fear, and must with horror fall,
And destin'd unto judgment, after all.
I feel my griefs too, and there scarce is ground
Upon my flesh t' inflict another wound.
Yet dare I not complain, or wish for death
With holy Paul, lest it be thought the breath
Of discontent; or that these prayers be
For weariness of life, not love of thee.

Ben Jonson (1572–1637)

BORN BY THE HOLY SPIRIT'S BREATH
(Based on selected verses from Romans 8)

Born by the Holy Spirit's breath,
loosed from the law of sin and death,
now cleared in Christ from every claim
no judgment stands against our name.

In us the Spirit makes his home
that we in him may overcome;
Christ's risen life, in all its powers,
its all-prevailing strength, is ours.

Sons, then, and heirs of God most high,
we by his Spirit 'Father' cry;
that Spirit with our spirit shares
to frame and breathe our wordless prayers.

One is his love, his purpose one;
to form the likeness of his Son
in all who, called and justified,
shall reign in glory at his side.

Nor death nor life, or powers unseen,
nor height nor depth can come between;
we know through peril, pain and sword,
the love of God in Christ our Lord.

Timothy Dudley-Smith

[THE WISDOM OF THE WISE]
(1 Corinthians 1.18–25)

The one is self-sufficient, and dictates
The kind of God he will accept: God must
Be mighty, wise, a trifle ruthless, just,
Exempt from tears and weakness, human fates.
The other, a technician, vitiates
Sound judgment by a cautious, righteous crust,
Demands specific miracles (for trust,
No place), and heaven's power domesticates.
   The Most High God is not impressed; His plan
   Commits his Son to human frailty,
   Exposing arrogance, rejecting canned
   Displays – transcendent folly, wise decree.
All vain pretensions must be cut to size:
I will destroy the wisdom of the wise.

D. A. Carson

NOT FOR TONGUES OF
HEAVEN'S ANGELS
(Based on 1 Corinthians 13)

Not for tongues of heaven's angels,
not for wisdom to discern,
not for faith that masters mountains,
for this better gift we yearn:
 may love be ours, O Lord.

Love is humble, love is gentle,
love is tender, true and kind;
love is gracious, ever patient,
generous of heart and mind:
 may love be ours, O Lord.

Never jealous, never selfish,
love will not rejoice in wrong;
never boastful nor resentful,
love believes and suffers long:
 may love be ours, O Lord.

In the day this world is fading
faith and hope will play their part;
but when Christ is seen in glory
love shall reign in every heart:
 may love be ours, O Lord.

Timothy Dudley-Smith

GOD FELT AND KNOWN
(God is in you of a truth – 1 Corinthians 14.25
Christ is in you – 2 Corinthians 13.5
The Spirit . . . dwelleth with you, and shall be in you – John 14.17)

God of a truth in us resides,
 Christ is in us both felt and known,
In us the Holy Ghost abides:
 Not three indwelling Gods, but one,
One true essential Deity
For ever one in persons three.

Charles Wesley

HOLY SONNETS:
DEATH, BE NOT PROUD
(Probably based on 1 Corinthians 15)

Death, be not proud, though some have called thee
Mighty and dreadful, for thou art not so;
For those whom thou think'st thou dost overthrow,
Die not, poor Death, nor yet can'st thou kill me.
From rest and sleep, which but thy pictures be,
Much pleasure; then from thee much more must flow,
And soonest our best men with thee do go,
Rest of their bones, and soul's delivery.
Thou art slave to fate, chance, kings, and desperate men,
And dost with poison, war, and sickness dwell;
And poppy or charms can make us sleep as well
And better than thy stroke; why swell'st thou then?
One short sleep past, we wake eternally,
And death shall be no more; Death, thou shalt die.

John Donne

[PAUL'S BOAST]
(2 Corinthians 11.23–30)

Credentials apostolic: here's my boast,
Certificate of God's elusive call.
I might have pointed out that I am Paul,
A Benjamite of purest lines, the toast
Of high rabbinic educators, most
Experienced church planter; but the pall
Of guilt, the grace of God, Golgotha – all
Combine to prompt this apostolic boast:
    Like wretched slaves I've worked – and borne the lash.
    Severely beaten, stoned, and shipwrecked thrice,
    In constant danger, treated like old trash
    By my own flocks – these prove I serve the Christ.
For I delight to suffer weakness, wrong.
Grace answers need; and when I'm weak, I'm strong.

D. A. Carson

FRUITFUL TREES, THE SPIRIT'S SOWING

(Based on Galatians 5.22, 23)

Fruitful trees, the Spirit's sowing,
may we ripen and increase,
fruit to life eternal growing,
rich in love and joy and peace.

Laden branches freely bearing
gifts the Giver loves to bless;
here is fruit that grows by sharing,
patience, kindness, gentleness.

Rooted deep in Christ our Master,
Christ our pattern and our goal,
teach us, as the years fly faster,
goodness, faith and self-control.

Fruitful trees, the Spirit's tending,
may we grow till harvests cease;
till we taste, in life unending,
heaven's love and joy and peace.

Timothy Dudley-Smith

OF IMPUTED RIGHTEOUSNESS

(Based on Ephesians 2.8, 9 and many other Scriptures)

Now, if thou wouldst inherit righteousness,
And so sanctification possess
In body, soul, and spirit, then thou must
To Jesus fly, as one ungodly first;
And so by him crave pardon for thy sin
Which thou hast loved, and hast lived in;
For this cannot at all forgiven be,
For any righteousness that is in thee;
Because the best thou hast is filthy rags,
Profane, presumptuous, and most beastly brags

Of flesh and blood, which always cross doth lie
To God, to grace, and thy felicity.

Then righteousness imputed thou must have,
Thee from that guilt and punishment to save
Thou liest under as a sinful man,
Throughout polluted, and that never can
By any other means acquitted be,
Or ever have true holiness in thee.
The reason is, because all graces are
Only in Christ, and be infused where,
Or into those whom he doth justify,
By what himself hath done, that he thereby
Might be the whole of all that happiness
The sinner shall enjoy here, and in bliss.

Besides, if holiness should first be found
In those whom God doth pardon, then the ground
Why we forgiven are would seem to be,
He first found holiness in thee and me;
But this the holy Scriptures will refute,
And prove that righteousness he doth impute
Without respect to goodness first in man;
For, to speak truth indeed, no goodness can
Be found in those that underneath the law
Do stand; for if God goodness in them saw,
Why doth he once and twice say, There is none
That righteous be; no, not so much as one;
None understandeth, none seek after God,
His ways they have not known, but have abode
In wickedness, unprofitably they
Must needs appear to be then every way.

Their throats an open sepulchre, also
Their mouths are full of filthy cursings too;
And bitterness, yea, underneath their lips
The asp hath poison. O how many slips
And falls in sin must such poor people have!
Now here's the holiness that should them save,
Or, as a preparation, go before,
To move God to do for them less or more?

No, grace must on thee righteousness bestow,
Or, else sin will for ever thee undo.
Sweet Paul this doctrine also doth express,
Where he saith, Some may have righteousness,
Though works they have not; and it thus may stand,
Grace by the promise gives what the command
Requireth us to do, and so are we
Quitted from doing, and by grace made free.

John Bunyan

THE SPRING OF BLESSING
(Ephesians 4.7–12)

The Saviour, when to heaven he rose,
In splendid triumph o'er his foes,
Scattered his gifts on men below,
And wide his royal bounties flow.

Hence sprung the Apostles' honoured name;
Sacred beyond heroic fame:
In lowlier forms before our eyes,
Pastors from hence, and teachers rise.

From Christ their varied gifts derive,
And fed by Christ their graces live:
While guarded by his mighty hand,
Midst all the rage of hell they stand.

So shall the bright succession run
Through the last courses of the sun;
While unborn churches by their care
Shall rise and flourish large and fair.

Jesus, now teach our hearts to know
The spring whence all these blessings flow;
Pastors and people shout thy praise
Through the long round of endless days.

Philip Doddridge (1702–51)

MEEKNESS AND MAJESTY
(Based on John 3.13–16 and Philippians 2.6–11)

Meekness and majesty,
manhood and deity
in perfect harmony –
the man who is God:
Lord of eternity
dwells in humanity,
kneels in humility
and washes our feet.

Oh what a mystery –
meekness and majesty:
bow down and worship,
for this is your God,
this is your God.

Father's pure radiance,
perfect in innocence,
yet learns obedience
to death on a cross:
suffering to give us life,
conquering through sacrifice –
and, as they crucify,
prays, 'Father, forgive.'

Wisdom unsearchable,
God the invisible,
love indestructible
in frailty appears:
Lord of infinity,
stooping so tenderly,
lifts our humanity
to the heights of his throne.

Graham Kendrick

THINK UPON THE LOVELY THINGS
(Philippians 4.8)

Think upon the lovely things,
    Set your mind on these;
Justice, truth, and purity,
    Godly qualities.

If there be virtue, any praise,
    Pray and do not be sad.
What's true, good, righteous,
    lovely, and pure,
Sing, praise God and be glad.

Meditate upon His Word,
    If you'd cleanse your path;
Make your needs well known to Him,
    Christ is your every breath.

Thoughts about the better things,
    Lead you to the best;
You will find it wonderful,
    Set your mind on Christ.

Linette Martin

PRAISE BE TO CHRIST
(Based on Colossians 1.15–20)

Praise be to Christ in whom we see
        the image of the Father shown,
        the first-born Son revealed and known,
    the truth and grace of deity;
through whom creation came to birth,
        whose fingers set the stars in place,
    the unseen powers, and this small earth,
        the furthest bounds of time and space.

Praise be to him whose sovereign sway
    and will upholds creation's plan;
    who is, before all worlds began
and when our world has passed away:
Lord of the church, its life and head,
    redemption's price and source and theme,
alive, the first-born from the dead,
    to reign as all-in-all supreme.

Praise be to him who, Lord most high,
    the fulness of the Godhead shares;
    and yet our human nature bears,
whom came as man to bleed and die.
And from his cross there flows our peace
    who chose for us the path he trod,
that so might sins and sorrows cease
    and all be reconciled to God.

Timothy Dudley-Smith

[I WONDER]
(Colossians 2.9; Deuteronomy 29.29; Job 38.1–7, 42.1–3)

I understand that matter can be changed
To energy; that maths can integrate
The complex quantum jumps that must relate
The fusion of the stars to history's page.
I understand that God in every age
Is Lord of all; that matter can't dictate;
That stars and quarks and all things intricate
Perform his word – including fool and sage.
    But knowing God is not to know like God;
    And science is a quest in infancy.
    Still more: transcendence took on flesh and blood –
    I do not understand how this can be.
The more my mind assesses what it can,
The more it learns the finitude of man.

D. A. Carson

SORROW, NOT WITHOUT HOPE
(1 Thessalonians 4.13–18)

Take comfort, Christians, when your friends
    In Jesus fall asleep;
Their better being never ends;
    Why then dejected weep?

Why inconsolable, as those
    To whom no hope is giv'n?
Death is the messenger of peace
    And calls the soul to heav'n.

As Jesus dy'd and rose again
    Victorious from the dead;
So his disciples rise, and reign
    With their triumphant Head.

The time draws nigh, when from the clouds
    Christ shall with shouts descend,
And the last trumpet's awful voice
    The heav'ns and earth shall rend.

Then they who live shall changed be,
    And they who sleep shall wake;
The graves shall yield their ancient charge,
    And earth's foundations shake.

The saints of God from death set free,
    With joy shall mount on high;
The heav'nly host with praises loud
    Shall meet them in the sky.

Together to their Father's house
    With joyful hearts they go;
And dwell for ever with the Lord,
    Beyond the reach of woe.

A few short years of evil past,
    We reach the happy shore,
Where death-divided friends at last
    Shall meet, to part no more.

Michael Bruce

GOING ONWARD
(2 Timothy 2.3)

Oft in danger, oft in woe,
Onward, Christians, onward go;
Fight the fight, maintain the strife,
Strengthened with the bread of life.

Let your drooping hearts be glad;
March in heavenly armour clad:
Fight, nor think the battle long,
Soon shall victory tune your song.

Let not sorrow dim your eye,
Soon shall every tear be dry;
Let not fears your course impede,
Great your strength if great your need.

Onward, then, to glory move,
More than conquerors ye shall prove;
Though opposed by many a foe,
Christian soldiers, onward go.

Henry Kirke White (1785–1806) and others

THE ENTHRONED HIGH PRIEST
(Hebrews 4.14–16)

Where high the heav'nly temple stands,
The house of God not made with hands,
A great High Priest our nature wears,
The guardian of mankind appears.

He who for men their surety stood
And pour'd on earth his precious blood
Pursues in heav'n his mighty plan
The Saviour and the friend of man.

Though now ascended up on high
He bends on earth a brother's eye;
Partaker of the human name
He knows the frailty of our frame.

Our fellow-suff'rer yet retains
A fellow-feeling of our pains;
And still remembers in the skies
His tears, his agonies and cries.

In ev'ry pang that rends the heart,
The Man of Sorrows had a part;
He sympathizes with our grief
And to the suff'rer sends relief.

With boldness therefore at the throne
Let us make all our sorrows known;
And ask the aids of heav'nly pow'r
To help us in the evil hour.

Michael Bruce

SOMETIMES I FEEL LIKE
A MOTHERLESS CHILD

Sometimes I feel like a motherless child,
A long ways from home.
True believer, true believer,
A long ways from home.

Sometimes I feel like I'm almost gone,
Way up in de Heb'nly land.
True believer, true believer,
Way up in de Heb'nly land.

Sometimes I feel like I'm almost gone,
Way up in de Heb'nly land.

Traditional Black American Spiritual

EXILE

Yes, it is beautiful country,
the streams in the winding valley,
the knowes and the birches,
and beautiful the mountain's bare shoulder
and the calm brows of the hills,
but it is not my country,
and in my heart there is a hollow place always.

And there is no way to go back –
maybe the miles indeed, but the years never.

Winding are the roads that we choose,
and inexorable is life,
driving us, it seems, like cattle
farther and farther away from what we remember.

But when we shall come at last
to God, who is our Home and Country,
there will be no more road stretching before us
and no more need to go back.
Evangeline Paterson (1928–2000)

knowe: knoll, mound, small hill

I'M A-ROLLING

O brothers, won't you help me?
O brothers, won't you help me to pray?
O brothers, won't you help me,
Won't you help me in the service of the Lord?

O sisters, won't you help me?
O sisters, won't you help me to pray?
O sisters, won't you help me,
Won't you help me in the service of the Lord?

O preachers, won't you help me?
O preachers, won't you help me to pray?
O preachers, won't you help me,
Won't you help me in the service of the Lord?

I'm a-rolling,
I'm a-rolling thro' an unfriendly world,
I'm a-rolling,
I'm a-rolling thro' an unfriendly world.

Traditional Black American Spiritual

DON'T BE WEARY, TRAVELLER

My head was wet with the midnight dew,
Come along home, come home,
The mornin' star was a witness too.
Come along home, come home.

Keep agoin', traveller,
Come along home, come home.
Keep a singin' all the way,
Come along home, come home.

Jes' where to go I did not know,
Come along home, come home.
A trav'lin' long and a trav'lin' slow,
Come along home, come home.

Don't be weary, traveller,
Come along home, come home.
Don't be weary, traveller,
Come along home, come home.

Traditional Black American Spiritual

A LIFE LOOKING UP TO THEE
(Hebrews 12.2)

Author of faith, appear!
Be thou its finisher;
Upward still for this we gaze,
Till we feel the stamp divine,
Thee behold with open face,
Bright in all thy glory shine.

Leave not thy work undone,
But ever love thine own;
Let us all thy goodness prove,
Let us to the end believe;
Show thine everlasting love,
Save us, to the utmost save.

O that our life might be
One looking up to thee!
Ever hasting to the day
When our eyes shall see thee near;
Come, Redeemer, come away,
Glorious in thy saints appear.

Charles Wesley

THE SECRET OF BLESSING
(See James 1.9–12)

Let every brother of a low degree
Rejoice in that he is advanced, but he
That's rich in being made low, for he shall pass
Away, as doth the flower of the grass.
For as the grass, soon as the sun doth rise,
Is scorched by reason of the heat, and dies;
Its flower fades, and it retains no more
The beauteous comeliness it had before,
So fades the rich man, maugre all his store.
The man is blest that doth endure temptation
For when he's tried, the crown of God's salvation,
The which the Lord hath promised to give
To them that love him, that man shall receive.

John Bunyan

PURE RELIGION
(See James 1.22–27)

Receive with meekness the engrafted word,
Which can salvation to your souls afford.
But be ye doers of the word each one,
And not deceive yourselves to hear alone;
For he that hears the word and doth it not,
Is like unto a man that hath forgot
What kind of man he was, though in a glass
He just before beheld his natural face.
But whoso minds the law of liberty
In its perfection, and continually
Abides therein, forgets not what he's heard,
But doth the work and therein hath reward.
If any man among you seem to be
Religious, he deceives himself if he
Doth not his tongue as with a bit restrain;
And all that man's religion is but vain.
Religion, pure and undefiled, which is
Acceptable before the Lord, is this:
To visit widows and the fatherless,
In time of their affliction or distress;
And so to regulate his conversation,
As to be spotless in his generation.

John Bunyan

TRUE WISDOM
(See James 3.17–18)

But the true wisdom that is from above,
Is, in the first place, pure, then full of love,
Then gentle and entreated easily,
Next merciful, without partiality,
Full of good fruits, without hypocrisy.
And what is more, the fruits of righteousness
Is sown in peace, of them that do make peace.

John Bunyan

PRACTICAL WISDOM
(See James 5.13–18)

Let him sing psalms that's merry; he that's grieved,
Let him by prayer seek to be relieved.
If any of you by sickness be distressed,
Let him the elders of the church request
That they would come and pray for him a while;
Anointing him in the Lord's name with oil;
So shall the pray'r that is of faith restore
The sick, and God shall raise him as before.
And all th' offences which he hath committed
Shall be forgiv'n, and he shall be acquitted.
Confess your faults each one unto his brother,
And put up supplications for each other,
That so you may be healed; the fervency
Of just men's prayers prevails effectually.
Elias was a man as frail as we are,
And he was earnest with the Lord in prayer,
That there might be no rain, and for the space
Of three years and six months no rain there was:
And afterward, when he again made suit,
The heaven gave rain, the earth brought forth her fruit.

John Bunyan

IS ANY SICK AMONG YOU?
(James 5.14)

Dear Lord, for all in pain
We pray to Thee
O come and smite again
Thine enemy.

Give to Thy servants skill
To soothe and bless,
And to the tired and ill
Give quietness.

And, Lord, to those who know
Pain may not cease,
Come near, that even so
They may have peace.

Anon.

CASTING ALL YOUR CARE UPON GOD,
FOR HE CARETH FOR YOU
(1 Peter 5.7)

Come, heavy souls, oppressed that are
With doubts, and fears, and carking care.
Lay all your burthens down and see
Where's One that carried once a tree
Upon His back, and, which is more,
A heavier weight, your sins, He bore.
Think then how easily He can
Your sorrows bear that's God and Man;
Think too how willing He's to take
Your care on Him, Who for your sake
Sweat bloody drops, prayed, fasted, cried,
Was bound, scourged, mocked and crucified.
He that so much for you did do,
Will do yet more, and care for you.

Thomas Washbourne (1606–87)

carking: burdensome, anxious

THE WORLD
(Based on 1 John 2.16–17)

I saw Eternity the other night,
Like a great ring of pure and endless light,
All calm, as it was bright;
And round beneath it, Time in hours, days, years,
Driv'n by the spheres
Like a vast shadow mov'd; in which the world
And all her train were hurl'd.

The doting lover in his quaintest strain
Did there complain;
Near him, his lute, his fancy, and his flights,
Wit's sour delights,
With gloves, and knots, the silly snares of pleasure,
Yet his dear treasure
All scatter'd lay, while he his eyes did pour
Upon a flow'r.

The darksome statesman hung with weights and woe,
Like a thick midnight-fog mov'd there so slow,
He did not stay, nor go;
Condemning thoughts (like sad eclipses) scowl
Upon his soul,
And clouds of crying witnesses without
Pursued him with one shout.
Yet digg'd the mole, and lest his ways be found,
Work'd under ground,
Where he did clutch his prey; but one did see
That policy;
Churches and altars fed him; perjuries
Were gnats and flies;
It rain'd about him blood and tears, but he
Drank them as free.

The fearful miser on a heap of rust
Sate pining all his life there, did scarce trust
His own hands with the dust,
Yet would not place one piece above, but lives
In fear of thieves;
Thousands there were as frantic as himself,
And hugg'd each one his pelf;
The downright epicure plac'd heav'n in sense,
And scorn'd pretence,
While others, slipp'd into a wide excess,
Said little less;
The weaker sort slight, trivial wares enslave,
Who think them brave;
And poor despised Truth sate counting by
Their victory.

Yet some, who all this while did weep and sing,
And sing, and weep, soar'd up into the ring;
But most would use no wing.
O fools (said I) thus to prefer dark night
Before true light,
To live in grots and caves, and hate the day
Because it shews the way,
The way, which from this dead and dark abode
Leads up to God,
A way where you might tread the sun, and be
More bright than he.
But as I did their madness so discuss
One whisper'd thus,
'This ring the Bridegroom did for none provide,
But for his bride.'

Henry Vaughan (1622?–95)

pelf: spoils, booty, possessions

[TO LOVE BOTH FREES AND BINDS]
(1 John 2.15–17)

To love both frees the lover from himself
And binds him to the loved; so to be loved
Is to become a god who stands above
The lover as the lover's choicest wealth.
But love's sweet freedom brings a double stealth,
An unseen chain, when god's the world, and love
Is lust, and pride of life's a grace: the loved,
This pampered god, is surreptitious self.
    A million billion trillion years from now,
    The gods pursued so hotly in our day
    Will find no selfish slaves to scrape and bow:
    The world and its desires all pass away.
Alone th'eternal God transforms, forgives:
And he who does God's will forever lives.

D. A. Carson

FOR A FRIEND DYING
(1 John 4.7–10)

When light broadens behind the curtains, and I wake
    to my peaceful morning,
my thoughts go at once to you, setting out in your slow
  day's business of dying.

In the midst of my life I am living your death, seeing
    with your eyes the shining
of sun on the leaf. All day I am keeping pace
    with your slow journey

and wishing that those you love may be there to send you
    – from love into Love going –
and may you launch out gently into the dark
    like keel into water moving.

Evangeline Paterson

THE
APOCALYPSE
(The Book of Revelation)

THE NEW DAY
(I was in the Spirit on the Lord's day – Revelation 1.10)

May I throughout this day of Thine
Be in Thy Spirit, Lord,
Spirit of humble fear divine
That trembles at Thy word,
Spirit of faith my heart to raise,
And fix on things above,
Spirit of sacrifice and praise,
Of holiness and love.

Charles Wesley (1707–88)

HE WALKS AMONG THE GOLDEN LAMPS
(Based on Revelation 1.12–18)

He walks among the golden lamps
on feet like burnished bronze;
his hair as snows of winter white,
his eyes with fire aflame, and bright
his glorious robe of seamless light
surpassing Solomon's.

And in his hand the seven stars
and from his mouth a sword:
his voice the thunder of the seas;
all creatures bow to his decrees
who holds the everlasting keys
and reigns as sovereign Lord.

More radiant than the sun at noon,
who was, and is to be:
who was, from everlasting days;
who lives, the Lord of all our ways;
to him be majesty and praise
for all eternity.

Timothy Dudley-Smith

SARDIS
(Revelation 3.1–6)

'Write to Sardis,' saith the Lord,
And write what he declares,
He whose Spirit, and whose word,
Upholds the seven stars:
'All thy works and ways I search,
Find thy zeal and love decay'd:
Thou art call'd a living church,
But thou art cold and dead.

'Watch, remember, seek, and strive,
Exert thy former pains;
Let thy timely care revive,
And strengthen what remains:
Cleanse thine heart, thy works amend
Former times to mind recall,
Lest my sudden stroke descend,
And smite thee once for all.

'Yet I number now in thee
A few that are upright;
These my Father's face shall see,
And walk with me in white.
When in judgment I appear,
They for mine shall be confest;
Let my faithful servants hear,
And woe be to the rest!'

William Cowper

SOMEBODY'S KNOCKIN' AT YOUR DOOR
(Revelation 3.20)

O sinner, why don't you answer?
Somebody's knockin' at your door!

Knocks like Jesus,
Somebody's knockin' at your door,
O sinner, why don't you answer?
Somebody's knockin' at your door!

Can't you hear him?
Somebody's knockin' at your door,
O sinner, why don't you answer?
Somebody's knockin' at your door!

Can't you trust him?
Somebody's knockin' at your door,
O sinner, why don't you answer?
Somebody's knockin' at your door!

Traditional Black American Spiritual

THE DAY OF WRATH
(Revelation 6.14)

The day of wrath, that dreadful day,
When heaven and earth shall pass away:
What power shall be the sinner's stay?
How shall he meet that dreadful day?

When, shrivelling like a parched scroll,
The flaming heavens together roll,
And louder yet, and yet more dread,
Swells the high trump that wakes the dead;

O! on that day, that aweful day,
When man to judgment wakes from clay,
Be thou, O Christ! the sinner's stay,
Though heaven and earth shall pass away.

Sir Walter Scott (1771–1832)

GWINE-A STUDY WAR NO MO'!

Gwine-a lay down mah burden,
Down by de ribberside,
Gwine-a lay down mah burden,
Down by de ribberside,
To study war no mo'!

I'm gwine-a study war no mo',
Ain't gwine-a study war no mo'!
I'm gwine-a put on mah long white robe,
Gwine-a put on mah starry crown,
Gwine-a study war no mo'!

Gwine-a lay down mah sword an' shield,
Down by de ribberside,
Gwine-a lay down mah sword an' shield,
Down by de ribberside,
To study war no mo'!

I'm gwine-a study war no mo',
Ain't gwine-a study war no mo'!
I'm gwine-a lay down mah sword an' shield,
Gwine-a put on mah starry crown,
Gwine-a study war no mo'!

Traditional Black American Spiritual

WHEN I'M GONE

When I'm gone,
Doan' yer grieve after me,
Bye an' bye,
Doan' yer grieve after me.

Pale horse an' rider done carry ma mother away;
Pale horse an' rider done carry ma sister away;
Cole icy han' done carry ma father away,
Bye an' bye; doan' yer grieve after me.

Traditional Black American Spiritual

IN DAT DAY

When you hear the thunder rollin',
In dat day, in dat day,
O sinner, why will you die in dat day?

When you see the rocks a-rendin',
In dat day, in dat day,
O sinner, why will you die in dat day?

When you feel the earth a-reelin',
In dat day, in dat day.
O sinner, why will you die in dat day?

When you see the moon a-bleedin',
In dat day, in dat day,
O sinner, why will you die in dat day?

When you hear the trump a-callin',
In dat day, in dat day,
O sinner, why will you die in dat day?

Traditional Black American Spiritual

THERE IS A LAND OF PURE DELIGHT

There is a land of pure delight,
Where saints immortal reign,
Infinite day excludes the night,
And pleasures banish pain.

There everlasting spring abides,
And never-withering flowers:
Death, like a narrow sea, divides
This heavenly land from ours.

Sweet fields beyond the swelling flood
Stand dressed in living green:
So to the Jews old Canaan stood,
While Jordan rolled between.

But timorous mortals start and shrink
To cross this narrow sea;
And linger, shivering on the brink,
And fear to launch away.

Isaac Watts (1674–1748)

GOIN' TO SHOUT

I got a robe, you got a robe,
All of God's children got a robe;
When I get to heav'n goin' to put on my robe,
Goin' to shout all over God's heav'n.
Heav'n, heav'n,
Ev'rybody talkin' 'bout heav'n ain't goin' there,
Heav'n, heav'n,
Goin' to shout all over God's heav'n.

I got a harp, you got a harp,
All of God's children got a harp;
When I get to heav'n goin' to play on my harp,
Goin' to play all over God's heav'n.
Heav'n, heav'n,
Ev'rybody talkin' 'bout heav'n ain't goin' there,
Heav'n, heav'n,
Goin' to play all over God's heav'n.

I got a shoes, you got a shoes,
All of God's children got a shoes;
When I get to heav'n goin' to put on my shoes,
Goin' to walk all over God's heav'n.
Heav'n, heav'n,
Ev'rybody talkin' 'bout heav'n ain't goin' there,
Heav'n, heav'n,
Goin' to shout all over God's heav'n.

Traditional Black American Spiritual

'THEY REST FROM THEIR LABOURS, AND THEIR WORKS DO FOLLOW THEM'
(Revelation 14.13)

The saints who die of Christ possest
Enter into immediate rest;
For them no further test remains,
Of purging fires, and torturing pains.

Who trusting in their Lord depart,
Cleansed from all sin, and pure in heart,
The bliss unmixed, the glorious prize,
They find with Christ in paradise.

Close followed by their works they go,
Their Master's purchased joy to know;
Their works enhance the bliss prepared,
And each hath its distinct reward.

Yet, glorified by grace alone,
They cast their crowns before the throne;
And fill the echoing courts above
With praises of redeeming love.

Charles Wesley

OH, WHEN I GET TO HEAVEN

Oh, when I get to heav'n goin' to set right down,
Ask my Lord for a starry crown,
Settin' down side of the Holy Lamb.

Peter, ring them bells,
Settin' down side of the Holy Lamb,
Save my soul from hell,
Settin' down side of the Holy Lamb.

Oh, when I get to heav'n goin' to ease, ease,
Me an' my God goin' to do as we please,
Settin' down side of the Holy Lamb,

Lordy is it true,
Settin down side of the Holy Lamb,
No more work to do!
Settin' down side of the Holy Lamb.

Traditional Black American Spiritual

BATTLE-HYMN OF THE REPUBLIC

Mine eyes have seen the glory of the coming of the Lord:
He is trampling out the vintage where the grapes of wrath are stored;
He hath loosed the fateful lightning of his terrible swift sword:
    His truth is marching on.

I have seen Him in the watch-fires of a hundred circling camps:
They have builded Him an altar in the evening dews and damps;
I can read his righteous sentence by the dim and flaring lamps,
    His day is marching on.

He has sounded forth the trumpet that shall never call retreat;
He is sifting out the hearts of men before his judgment seat;
Oh! be swift, my soul, to answer Him; be jubilant, my feet!
    Our God is marching on.

In the beauty of the lilies Christ was born across the sea,
With a glory in his bosom that transfigures you and me:
As He died to make men holy, let us die to make men free,
    While God is marching on.

Julia Ward Howe (1819–1910)

BLOW YOUR TRUMPET, GABRIEL

De talles' tree in Paradise,
De Christian call de tree of life,
An' I hope dat trump will blow me home
To my New Jerusalem.

De talles' tree in Paradise,
De Christian call de tree of life,
An' I hope dat trump will blow me home
To my New Jerusalem.

So blow de trumpet, Gabriel,
Blow de trumpet,
An' I hope dat trump will blow me home
To my New Jerusalem.

O Paul and Silas bound in jail,
Sing God's praises night and day,
An' I hope dat trump will blow me home
To my New Jerusalem.

So blow de trumpet, Gabriel,
Blow de trumpet,
An' I hope dat trump will blow me home
To my New Jerusalem.

Traditional Black American Spiritual

THE GREAT ARCHANGEL'S TRUMP
SHALL SOUND

The great archangel's trump shall sound,
(While twice ten thousand thunders roar)
Tear up the graves, and cleave the ground,
And make the greedy sea restore.

The greedy sea shall yield her dead,
The earth no more her slain conceal;
Sinners shall lift their guilty head,
And shrink to see a yawning hell.

But we, who now our Lord confess,
And faithful to the end endure,
Shall stand in Jesu's righteousness,
Stand, as the Rock of ages, sure.

We, while the stars from heaven shall fall,
And mountains are on mountains hurled,
Shall stand unmoved amidst them all,
And smile to see a burning world.

The earth, and all the works therein,
Dissolve, by raging flames destroyed,
While we survey the awful scene,
And mount above the fiery void.

By faith we now transcend the skies,
And on that ruined world look down;
By love above all height we rise,
And share the everlasting throne.

Charles Wesley

MY LORD, WHAT A MORNIN'!

Oh, my Lord, what a mornin'
When the stars begin to fall.
You'll hear the trumpet sound
To wake the nations underground,
Look in my God's right hand,
When the stars begin to fall.

Oh, my Lord, what a mornin'
You'd hear the Christians shout,
To wake the nations underground,
Look in my God's right hand,
When the stars begin to fall.

Oh, my Lord, what a mornin'
When the stars begin to fall.
You'll hear the angels sing
To wake the nations underground,
Look in my God's right hand,
When the stars begin to fall.

Traditional Black American Spiritual

OF THE SPOUSE OF CHRIST

Who's this that cometh from the wilderness,
    Like smokey pillars thus perfum'd with myrrh,
Leaning upon her dearest in distress,
    Led into's bosom by the Comforter?
She's clothed with the sun, crowned with twelve stars,
    The spotted moon her footstool she hath made.
The dragon her assaults, fills her with jars,
    Yet rests she under her Beloved's shade,
But whence was she? what is her pedigree?
    Was not her father a poor Amorite?
What was her mother but as others be,
    A poor, a wretched, and a sinful Hittite.
Yea, as for her, the day that she was born,
    As loathsome, out of doors they did her cast;
Naked and filthy, stinking and forlorn;

This was her pedigree from first to last.
Nor was she pitied in this estate,
    All let her lie polluted in her blood:
None her condition did commiserate,
    There was no heart that sought to do her good.
Yet she unto these ornaments is come,
    Her breasts are fashioned, her hair is grown;
She is made heiress of the best kingdom;
    All her indignities away are blown.
Cast out she was, but now she home is taken,
    Naked (sometimes), but now, you see, she's cloth'd;
Now made the darling, though before forsaken,
    Barefoot, but now as princes' daughters shod.
Instead of filth, she now has her perfumes;
    Instead of ignominy, her chains of gold:
Instead of what the beauty most consumes,
    Her beauty's perfect, lovely to behold.
Those that attend and wait upon her be
    Princes of honour, clothed in white array;
Upon her head's a crown of gold, and she
    Eats wheat, honey, and oil, from day to day.
For her beloved, he's the high'st of all,
    The only Potentate, the King of kings:
Angels and men do him Jehovah call,
    And from him life and glory always springs.
He's white and ruddy, and of all the chief:
    His head, his locks, his eyes, his hands, and feet,
Do, for completeness, out-go all belief;
    His cheeks like flowers are, his mouth most sweet.
As for his wealth, he is made heir of all;
    What is in heaven, what is on earth is his:
And he this lady his joint-heir doth call,
    Of all that shall be, or at present is.
Well, lady, well, God has been good to thee;
    Thou of an outcast, now art made a queen.
Few, or none, may with thee compared be,
    A beggar made thus high is seldom seen.
Take heed of pride, remember what thou art
    By nature, though thou hast in grace a share,
Thou in thyself dost yet retain a part
    Of thine own filthiness; wherefore beware.

John Bunyan

THE SECOND COMING

If I had known it was he
I would not have answered.
The time just wasn't right.
It was Christmas
and half of the tea
servant girls
lay sleeping, drunk.
And besides,
the mistress was busy,
you know, celebrating.
He strode in, beaming
with that radiant smile of his
and asked for her.
I thought to tell him
'She is out' or
'She is not quite ready' or
'I'll just go and see'
but, being just a servant,
I hesitated,
and he bounded up the stairs
with a joyful cry,
anticipating the joy
of his beloved.
I heard him fling the door open.
They were just . . .
I heard her scream
that she was sorry
that this other
had forced his way.
He stumbled down the stairs
and through the still-open door
back to the cold and silent darkness.
And he wept.

David Waltner-Toews (b. 1948)

OF HEAVEN
(An extract)

That head that once was crown'd with thorns,
Shall now with glory shine;
That heart that broken was with scorns,
Shall flow with life divine;

That man that here met with disgrace,
We there shall see so bright;
That angels can't behold his face
For its exceeding light.

What gladness will possess our heart
When we shall see these things!
What light and life, in every part,
Will rise like lasting springs!

O blessed face and holy grace,
When shall we see this day?
Lord, fetch us to this goodly place
We humbly do thee pray.

This shall we see, thus shall we be,
O would the day were come,
Lord Jesus take us up to thee,
To this desired home.

John Bunyan

HIERUSALEM

Hierusalem my happy home
When shall I come to thee
When shall my sorrows have an end
Thy joys when shall I see

O happy harbour of the saints
O sweet and pleasant soil
In thee no sorrow may be found
No grief, no care, no toil

In thee no sickness may be seen
No hurt, no ache, no sore
There is no death, nor ugly devil
There is life for evermore

No dampish mist is seen in thee
No cold, nor darksome night
There every soul shines as the sun
There God himself gives light

There lust and lucre cannot dwell
There envy bears no sway
There is no hunger, heat nor cold
But pleasure every way

Hierusalem: Hierusalem
God grant I once may see
Thy endless joys and of the same
Partaker aye to be

Thy walls are made of precious stones
Thy bulwarks Diamonds square
Thy gates are of right orient pearl
Exceeding rich and rare

Thy turrets and thy pinnacles
With carbuncles do shine
Thy very streets are paved with gold
Surpassing clear and fine

Thy houses are of Ivory
Thy windows crystal clear
Thy tiles are made of beaten gold
O God that I were there

Within thy gates nothing doth come
That is not passing clean
No spiders web, no dirt nor dust
No filth may there be seen

Ah my sweet home Hierusalem
Would God I were in thee

Would God my woes were at an end
Thy joys that I might see

Thy saints are crowned with glory great
They see God face to face
They triumph still, they still rejoice
Most happy is their case

We that are here in banishment
Continually do mourn
We sigh and sob, we weep and wail
Perpetually we groan

Our sweet is mixed with bitter gall
Our pleasure is but pain
Our joys scarce last the looking on
Our sorrows still remain

But there they live in such delight
Such pleasure and such play
As that to them a thousand years
Doth seem as yesterday

Thy vineyards and thy orchards are
Most beautiful and faire
Full furnished with trees and fruits
Most wonderful and rare

Thy gardens and thy gallant walks
Continually are green
There grows such sweet and pleasant flowers
As nowhere else are seen

There is nectar and ambrosia made
There is musk and civet sweet
There many a fair and dainty drug
Are trodden under feet

There cinnamon there sugar grows
There nard and balm abound
What tongue can tell or heart conceive
The joys that there are found

Quiet through the streets with silver sound
The flood of life doth flow
Upon whose banks on every side
The wood of life doth grow

There trees for evermore bear fruit
And evermore do springs
There evermore the Angels sit
And evermore do sing

There David stands with harp in hand
As master of the Quire
Ten thousand times that man were blest
That might this music hear

Our Lady sings magnificat
With tune surpassing sweet
And all the virgins hear their parts
Sitting about her feet

Te Deum doth Saint Ambrose sing
Saint Augustine doth the like
Old Simeon and Zacharie
Have not their songs to seek

There Magdalene hath left her moan
And cheerfully doth sing
With blessed Saints whose harmony
In every street doth ring

Hierusalem my happy home
Would God I were in thee
Would God my woes were at an end
Thy joys that I might see

finis   finis
FBP (Anon. c. 1580)

Hierusalem: Jerusalem

ACKNOWLEDGEMENTS
AND SOURCES

W. H. Auden, 'At the Manger Mary Sings', from 'For the Time Being: A Christmas Oratorio', *Collected Longer Poems*, Faber & Faber Ltd, 1968. Used by permission of Faber & Faber Ltd and Random House Inc.

Margaret Avison, 'The Dumbfounding', 'The Word' and 'Ps. 19', from *The Dumbfounding*. Copyright © 1966 by Margaret Avison. Used by permission of W. W. Norton & Company, Inc.

John Bunyan, 'Jonah Flees from God', from *The Prophecy of Jonah*. 'Potiphar's Wife', from *The Life of Joseph*. 'Practical Wisdom', 'The Secret of Blessing', 'Pure Religion' and 'True Wisdom', from *The General Epistle of James*. 'Samson and Delilah', from *The History of Samson*.

Amy Carmichael, 'Shadow and Coolness', from *Edges of His Ways*, © 1955 The Dohnavur Fellowship. Published by Christian Literature Crusade, Fort Washington, PA. Used by permission.

D. A. Carson, '[I wonder]', Sonnet Forty, '[Paul's boast]', Sonnet Forty-four, '[The stranger]' Sonnet Twenty-nine, '[To love both frees and binds]', Sonnet Forty-six and '[The wisdom of the wise]', Sonnet Forty-one, from *Holy Sonnets of the Twentieth Century*, Baker Books/Crossway Books Ltd, 1994.

Jack Clemo, 'The Winds', from *The Map of Clay*, Methuen, 1961.

Edmund P. Clowney, 'The Singing Christ'. Used by permission of the author.

William Cowper, 'Sardis' and 'Wisdom', from *The Olney Hymns*, by William Cowper and John Newton.

Richard Crashaw, 'Samson to his Delilah', from *Divine Epigrams*.

'A Dream of the Cross (Dream of the Rood)', edited and translated by Charles W. Kennedy, *Early English Christian Poetry*, New York, Oxford University Press, 1963. Used by permission of Oxford University Press Inc.

William Drummond of Hawthornden, 'On John the Baptist', from *The Flowers of Sin*.

Timothy Dudley-Smith, 'Beyond All Mortal Praise', 'Born by the Holy Spirit's Breath', 'Fruitful Trees, the Spirit's Sowing', 'He Walks Among the Golden Lamps', 'The Heavens Are Singing', 'I Lift My Eyes', 'In the Same Night In Which He Was Betrayed', 'Not For Tongues of Heaven's Angels', 'O God Who Brought the Light to Birth', 'O God Who Shaped the Starry Skies', 'Praise Be To Christ'. Used by permission of the author.

T. S. Eliot, 'Journey of the Magi', from *Collected Poems*. Used by permission of Faber & Faber Ltd and Harcourt Brace.

FBP (Anon.), 'Hierusalem', British Museum Additional Manuscripts 15,225.

Eleanor Farjeon, 'Joseph Fell a-Dreaming', from *Silver Sand and Snow*, Michael Joseph, 1951. 'Put On Your Purple, Esther', from *Eleanor Farjeon's Book*, Penguin, 1960. Used by permission of David Higham Associates.

Tom Gledhill, 'Another Dream of Frustration' and 'In Praise of His Beloved', from *The Bible Speaks Today: The Message of the Song of Songs*, IVP, 1994. Used by permission of Inter-Varsity Press.

John Heath-Stubbs, 'Two Poems for the Epiphany', from *Collected Poems 1943–1987*, Carcanet, 1988. Used by permission of David Higham Associates.

Stewart Henderson, 'There Was No'. Used by permission of the author.

Benjamin Keach, 'His Eyes Are Like the Eyes of Doves', from *A Feast of Fat Things*, 1696.

Carolyn Keefe, 'Easter'. Used by permission of the author.

Graham Kendrick, 'Meekness and Majesty', copyright © 1986 Thankyou Music, PO Box 75, Eastbourne, East Sussex BN23 6NW. 'The Servant King', copyright © 1983 Thankyou Music, PO Box 75, Eastbourne, East Sussex BN23 6NW.

Alison Leonard, 'Miriam'. Used by permission of the author.

C. S. Lewis, 'The Late Passenger', from *Poems*. Copyright © C. S. Lewis Pte. Ltd, 1964. Extract reprinted by permission.

Linette Martin, 'There is No Love On Earth As Great As Thine', 'Think Upon the Lovely Things' and 'Thou My Shield and Thou My Light'. Used by permission of The Estate of Linette Martin.

John Milton, 'The First Temptation', from *Paradise Regained* (Book I, lines 280–502). 'The Meeting of Adam and Eve', from *Paradise Lost* (Book VIII, lines 379–559).

John Henry Newman, 'The Pillar of Cloud', from *The Dream of Gerontius*.

'Of God', from *England's Parnassus*. Printed in London for NLCB and TH, 1600.

Evangeline Paterson, 'Exile' and 'For a Friend Dying'. Used by permission of Carolyn Rowland-Jones.

David J. Payne, 'God in the Desert' and 'The Ransomed of the Lord Return With Joy'. Used by permission of the author.

Eugene Peterson, 'John the Baptist'. Used by permission of the author.

John Piper, 'Rahab'. Used by permission of the author.

'The Rebellion and Fall of Lucifer', edited and translated by Charles W. Kennedy, *Early English Christian Poetry*, New York, Oxford University Press, 1963. Used by permission of Oxford University Press Inc.

Luci Shaw, ' . . . For They Shall See God', 'The Joining', and 'Mary's Song', from *Polishing the Petoskey Stone*, Shaw, 1976. Used by permission.

'The Ten Commandments', translated by Brian Stone, from *Medieval English Verse*, Penguin Classics, 1974. Copyright © Brian Stone 1964. Used by permission of Penguin UK.

John Updike, 'Seven Stanzas at Easter', from *Telephone Poles and Other Poems*. Copyright © 1961 by John Updike. Used by permission of Penguin UK and Alfred A. Knopf.

David Waltner-Toews, 'The Second Coming'. Used by permission of the author.

James Weldon Johnson, 'The Creation' and 'The Prodigal Son', from *God's Trombones*. Copyright © 1927 The Viking Press, Inc., renewed 1955 by Grace Nail Johnson. Used by permission of Viking Penguin, a division of Penguin Putnam Inc.

Veronica Zundel, 'A Quiet Roar'. Used by permission of the author.

The publisher and author thank those individuals and organizations that have given us permission to use and adapt material for this book. Every effort has been made to trace the owners of copyright material, though in a few cases this may not have been possible. We trust that where copyright material has been used without permission, the owners will contact us directly.

GLOSSARY

Alliterative verse A powerful poetry based more around the voice than instrumental music, and depending for its effect on alliteration and metre rather than rhyme. Such verse was common in Latin and the Celtic and Germanic languages, to which Early English poetry belongs. There are several examples in this collection, translated well into modern alliterative verse: *The Rebellion and Fall of Lucifer* (page 6, from *Genesis*) and *Dream of the Rood* (page 148). Some modern writers have effectively explored the potential of this type of poetry, including J. R. R. Tolkien, W. H. Auden and Gerard Manley Hopkins (in his invented sprung rhythm).

Ballad An oral narrative poem, usually anonymous, and often sung to a simple instrumental accompaniment. Many melodies have been preserved, but even more of the poems. The most important period of ballads was the late Middle Ages, where they particularly flourished in Lowland Scotland and the Border counties of England. A representative ballad is included in this collection, *Dives and Lazarus*, page 131.

The Creation This poem by James Weldon Johnson is based on folk sermons of the black American he heard in his boyhood. See his Preface to *God's Trombones* and his *Along this Way*. He likened the powerful voice of the old-time preacher to a trombone, and acknowledged the influence of the 'Negro' Spirituals on his poetry.

Dream of the Rood The earliest dream poem and one of the finest religious poems in the English language. Its author is unknown. In a dream he perceives a beautiful tree, which turns out to be the rood, or cross, on which Christ died. The rood tells its story. It had been forced to be the instrument of Jesus' death. Then it was horribly bloodstained but now it signifies Christ's glorious redemption. The complete version of the poem was discovered nearly 200 years ago in the tenth-century Vercelli Book, which had been taken to Italy.

Early English verse Early English describes the English language during the first millennium of its existence (approximately 450–1450). The early history of the English language includes Anglo-Saxon and then the Middle English period (from roughly the impact of the Norman Conquest until well into the fifteenth century), long before attempts to standardize the language. In this collection examples from Early English verse are mostly in translation, or contain helps on more obscure word forms. Examples include *The Rebellion and Fall of Lucifer*

213

(page 6, from *Genesis*), *Dream of the Rood* (page 148), and *Adam lay ibounden* (page 14). This period is very rich in Christian and biblical poetry, and its representation in this collection is very limited because of the necessity for translation or explanation. Because the Middle English poet Chaucer is still studied in secondary schools it is easy to find guides to the language of that period, particularly his dialect. It is worth considering studying Anglo-Saxon, in order to read the poetry and literature of the earlier period. An excellent textbook (which has an accompanying audiotape) is *First Steps in Old English* by Stephen Pollington (Anglo-Saxon Books, Hockwold-cum-Wilton, Norfolk, England (ISBN 1-898281-19-X)).

'Negro' Spirituals A number of these unsurpassed traditional American spirituals are included in this collection, born in the pain of slavery and its aftermath. Related to them are black sermon poems (see the included poems by Paul Laurence Dunbar and James Weldon Johnson).

Paradise Lost is generally regarded as the greatest epic poem in the English language, composed in 12 books of blank verse. It is represented in *The Poetic Bible* (see page 9). It tells the story of the creation of the world as paradise, the fall of Lucifer, and the subsequent fall of Adam and Eve. Its picture of a war in heaven before the fall of humanity, picking up of the imaginative possibilities of the talking serpent of Genesis 3, draws on a long tradition, including the Early English poem *Genesis*, an extract from which appears on page 6.

Paradise Regained This is a sequel to John Milton's *Paradise Lost*, in which the second Adam wins back for man what the first Adam had lost. It concentrates upon the theme of temptation, as Christ goes through his ordeal in the Wilderness. An extract appears on page 118.

Samson Agonistes This is the greatest English drama based upon the Greek model and is intended more for reading than performance. The play deals with the last phase of Samson's life. His blindness is even more poignant when one realizes that the poet himself was blind when composing the work. An extract appears on page 42.

Saul The first nine sections of *Saul* were first published in Robert Browning's *Dramatic Romances and Lyrics*. The complete poem first appeared in the second volume of his *Men and Women*. The poem is based upon 1 Samuel 18. Abner was 'the captain of the host'.

Scriptural Poems John Bunyan composed a collection of paraphrases in rhyming couplets of a number of biblical books, or sections. These included poems on the life of Joseph, Samson, Ruth, and Jonah, as well as the Beatitudes and the Epistle of James. Several extracts appear, for example, on pages 21, 43, 106 and 186.

POETS

Auden, W. H. (1907–73) Born in York, he grew up in Birmingham, and studied at Oxford. Later he lived in the United States, where he became a citizen. He was Professor of Poetry at Oxford University between 1956–60. His conversion to Christianity, after many years as a materialist, deeply affected his poetry and other writings.

Avison, Margaret (b. 1918) One of Canada's finest poets, she was born in Galt, Ontario and educated at the University of Toronto. Her collections include *Winter Sun* (1960), *The Dumbfounding* (1966) and *Sunblue* (1978).

Baldwin, William (sixteenth century) Employed as a proof-reader for a printer, he later became a school-teacher. He was known to have provided theatrical exhibitions for the court of Queen Mary, and composed metrical translations of Scripture.

Beaumont, Joseph (1615–99) Suffolk-born, he became Master of Peterhouse College, Cambridge in 1663.

Bonar, Horatius (1808–89) A Scottish hymn-writer who ministered at the Chalmers Memorial Church in Edinburgh.

Browning, Elizabeth Barrett (1806–61) After a childhood in Malvern and a period in Sidmouth, her family moved to Wimpole Street in 1838. A younger admirer of her poems, Robert Browning, secretly married her in 1846 because of her father's disapproval, and the couple moved to Italy. The publication of *Aurora Leigh* in 1856 established her reputation as a leading poet.

Browning, Robert (1812–69) He was an innovative, prolific and outstanding Victorian poet, husband of Elizabeth Barrett Browning.

Bruce, Michael (1746–67) Born in Kinnesswood, Kinross-shire, he was a Scottish poet who died very young and whose works show great promise. His parents gave him a good education, and he attended four winter sessions at the University of Edinburgh. In 1766 he wrote his last and most well-known poem, *Elegy Written in Spring*. A university friend and fellow poet, John Logan, published much of Michael Bruce's work under his own name after borrowing a manuscript from Bruce's unsuspecting father, and it was many years before the extent of his deception was fully realized. Michael Bruce wrote under the growing influence of Isaac Watts' hymns.

Bunyan, John (1628–88) Puritan pastor, preacher and writer, imprisoned for many years in Bedford gaol for his Nonconformism. His allegory, *The Pilgrim's Progress*, has been one of the widest read books in English literature.

Byron, George Noel Gordon, Lord (1788–1824) Though born in London, he grew up in Scotland. Aged ten he was left a barony and family home, Newstead Abbey, near Nottingham. He quit England in 1816, and famously joined Percy and Mary Shelley in Switzerland. He then moved on to Italy where he became attached to a Countess in Ravenna. He later supported the cause of Greek liberation from the Ottomans. After dying of rheumatic fever his body was returned to England but was refused burial in Westminster Abbey.

Carmichael, Amy W. (1867–1951) Missionary in India and author of many books. She founded the Dohnavur Fellowship, a pioneering rescue home for children. An accident in 1932 left her housebound.

Carson, D. A. (b. 1946) Research Professor of New Testament at Trinity Evangelical Divinity School. The Canadian has written major commentaries and works of theology covering personal Christian concerns, including *How Long, O Lord? Reflections on Suffering and Evil*. He is also popular as a preacher and conference speaker.

Clare, John (1793–1864) A rural poet who worked as a thresher, farm labourer and gardener in the area of Helpston, Northamptonshire. He suffered mental illness and spent the last part of his life in the county asylum. His poetry was rediscovered in the twentieth century after a long period of neglect.

Clemo, Jack (1916–74) Cornish poet inspired by a landscape of claypits. Deaf for 40 years, and blind for 25 of them, he found happiness in a late marriage. As well as a novel, *Wilding Graft*, he published many books of verse and an autobiography, *The Invading Gospel*.

Clough, Arthur Hugh (1819–61) A Liverpool-born poet, he was the child of a cotton merchant who emigrated to South Carolina. After spending his early years in the USA he returned to England and was educated at Rugby School and Balliol College, Oxford. Later he was for a period a tutor in Cambridge, Massachusetts, where he became friendly with Ralph Waldo Emerson. He is commemorated in his friend Matthew Arnold's poem, *Thyrsis*.

Clowney, Edmund P. (b. 1919) Formerly President of Westminster Theological Seminary, Philadelphia, he is now Associate Pastor of Christ the King Presbyterian Church, Houston, Texas.

Coleridge, Mary (1861–1907) A London-born poet and novelist, and great-granddaughter of Samuel Taylor Coleridge's brother.

The Countess of Pembroke, *see* **Herbert, Mary, The Countess of Pembroke**

Cowper, William (1731–1800) A leading poet of his day who struggled with mental illness. With his friend, John Newton, he contributed to the influential *Olney Hymns*. Predating the Romantic Movement Cowper introduced a directness to contemporary poetry. He enjoyed describing nature, and had a concern for the poor and marginalized, influenced by the Evangelical revival.

Crashaw, Richard (1612–49) The son of a well-known Puritan divine, he later turned to a Roman Catholic faith.

Davies, Sir John (1569–1626) A philosophic poet and politician who as an MP represented both English and Irish constituencies. He died the day before he was to become Lord Chief Justice of England.

Dickinson, Emily (1830–86) A fascinating recluse, mostly unpublished until after her death, she is one of America's greatest poets. She composed over a thousand poems in her distinctive style, marked by originality and subtlety of thought and a complex, interesting faith.

Doddridge, Philip (1702–51) A hymn-writer who was born in London and studied for the Nonconformist ministry at Kibworth Academy, Leicestershire. He died in Lisbon where he was staying in order to improve his health. His *The Rise and Progress of Religion in the Soul* (1745) was translated into many languages.

Donne, John (1572–1631) A poet of the Metaphysical school, who wrote memorable love poetry, and married for love. He was later ordained into the Church of England, becoming Dean of St Paul's, and a famous preacher.

Drummond, William of Hawthornden (1585–1649) A friend of Ben Jonson, who devoted his life to poetry and to mechanical experiments. His fiancée, Mary Cunningham, died on the eve of their wedding, and she inspired many songs and sonnets.

Dudley-Smith, Timothy (b. 1926) He was Secretary of the Church Pastoral Aid Society from 1965 to 1973, before moving to Norfolk to become Archdeacon of Norwich and Bishop of Thetford. He now lives and writes in Salisbury, England. He is the biographer of his friend, John Stott. Author of a number of books and anthologies he is best known as a hymn-writer, appearing in numerous hymnals. Recordings of his hymns appear all over the world.

Dunbar, Paul Laurence (1872–1906) The son of former slaves, he took standard black employment as an elevator operator while privately publishing two books of poetry. His break came when he was championed as a dialect poet. His protests were, in his words, 'mouth[ed] with myriad subtleties', revealed in the poem included here (*An Ante-Bellum Sermon*). His powerful poem, *We Wear a Mask*, confesses: 'We smile, but, O great Christ, our cries/To thee from tortured souls arise.' Fraught by ill-health and an unhappy marriage, he died of tuberculosis.

Eliot, T. S. (1888–1965) Poet, playwright, publisher and critic who was a leader in the modern movement. American-born, he became a British citizen and joined the Church of England.

Farjeon, Eleanor (1881–1965) A writer of fantasies and children's stories, and the popular song, *Morning Has Broken*. Daughter of an American mother and novelist father she began writing stories and verses at the age of six. In 1955 she was awarded The Carnegie Medal for a collection of children's stories, *The Little Bookroom*.

Fraser, Norman (b. 1962) grew up in the Scottish Highlands, soaked in the singing of metrical psalms from the Scottish Psalter. He has worked in higher education and business, and until recently was Assistant Head of Student Ministries at the Universities and Colleges Christian Fellowship, Great Britain.

Gledhill, Tom (b. 1942) After lecturing in Physics in universities in Malawi, Uganda, Turkey and Nigeria, he taught the Old Testament in Nairobi Evangelical Graduate School of Theology, Kenya. He now lectures in Biblical Studies at the Evangelical Theological College of Wales. He is author of *The Message of the Song of Songs* in IVP's *The Bible Speaks Today* series of expositions.

Heath-Stubbs, John (b. 1918) A poet, critic, anthologist and translator who has taught, worked in publishing, and held fellowships and professorial posts in three continents. He was awarded the Queen's Medal for Poetry in 1973, and has written studies of several writers, including Charles Williams.

Henderson, Stewart Liverpool-born, of a Scottish family, he is a performance poet, broadcaster and scriptwriter with eight books of verse published. His poetry has appeared in many anthologies and is studied by school children.

Herbert, Mary, The Countess of Pembroke (1561–1621) She was the sister of the poet Sir Philip Sidney, author of *An Apology for Poetry*. She was a patron of poets. After her brother's death she revised his *Arcadia*.

Howe, Julia Ward (1819–1910) A biographer and poet, she was a notable female suffrage leader. She promoted prison reform and international peace.

Johnson, James Weldon (1871–1938) He was educated at Atlanta University and Columbia, and was among the first to break through American racial barriers. He was the first black admitted to the Florida bar. As well as this role, he was at different times a songwriter in New York, American Consul in Nicaragua and Venezuela, and a lecturer in creative literature at Fisk University. His life is told in *Along this Way*. He also wrote a novel *The Autobiography of an Ex-Colored Man* (1912).

Jonson, Ben (1572–1637) He was a dramatist and poet who joined an acting company and killed a fellow actor in a duel. William Shakespeare acted in Jonson's play, *Every Man in His Humour*.

Keach, Benjamin (1640–1704) He was a Baptist pastor who ran foul of the authorities for his preaching and a publication. He also caused a schism by promoting congregation singing.

Keefe, Carolyn American educationalist, she has spoken and written widely on religious communication, forensic education, and C. S. Lewis as speaker and teacher. Now retired, she is Professor Emeritus of Communication Studies, West Chester University.

Kendrick, Graham (b. 1950) The son of a Baptist pastor, he was born in Northamptonshire. He trained as a teacher, but launched his career as a singer/songwriter in 1972. His song, *Shine, Jesus, Shine* is one of the UK's most popular contemporary worship songs. He is a member of the Ichthus Christian Fellowship, London, and a co-founder of March for Jesus. This prayer, praise and proclamation event became global on 25 June 1994, with over 12 million people from 177 nations taking to the streets to proclaim their faith.

Kennedy, Charles W. (1882–1969) A notable translator of early English poetry, and one-time Murray Professor of English Literature at Princeton University. His translations appear on pages 6 and 148.

Kethe, William (d. 1608?) He accompanied the Earl of Warwick to France as minister to the English army, 1563. He is famous for his metrical psalms, first published in the English Psalter of 1561.

Leonard, Alison (b. 1944) She grew up between the Anglican and Methodist Churches and, after almost becoming a Baha'i, joined the Religious Society of Friends (Quakers) as an adult. She writes fiction and drama for adults and children and has a particular interest in encouraging people to tell their spiritual stories in all their diversity and complexity.

Lewis, C. S. (1898–1963) Christian apologist, writer of fiction and poetry, and literary historian, who was the centre of the Inklings, a mainly Christian Oxford literary group that met informally, and included J. R. R. Tolkien and Charles Williams. His first book of poetry was published when he was 21, and an atheist.

Martin, Linette (1937–98) She was born Linette Brown and grew up near Guildford, Surrey. She trained as a dancer and danced professionally for a number of years in various places, including Glyndebourne. Linette was a worker at L'Abri Fellowship in Switzerland with Francis and Edith Schaeffer from 1959 to 1965. She wrote several books, including *Hans Rookmaaker: A Biography* and *Practical Praying*. She died in December 1998 after a valiant fight against cancer. Forthcoming books include *How to Read Icons*.

Melville, Herman (1819–91) One of America's greatest writers; novelist, poet, short-story writer, whose *Moby Dick* (1851) was a defining novel of American literature.

Milton, John (1608–74) One of the greatest English poets, and author of religious and political pamphlets, ranging from the subjects of freedom to a justification of divorce in certain circumstances. Much of his poetry was written after he became blind, including *Paradise Lost*, *Paradise Regained* and *Samson Agonistes*.

Newman, John Henry (1801–90) Famously converted to the Roman Catholic Church after being part of the Tractarian movement of the Church of England, becoming a cardinal.

Paterson, Evangeline (1928–2000) Her early life was passed in Limavady, Northern Ireland and Dublin. She married an English geographer and lived in Cambridge, St Andrews, Leicester and Newcastle. She was a founder and co-editor of the journal *Other Poetry*, a friend much missed.

Payne, David J. (b. 1931) After reading Natural Sciences at Clare College, Cambridge, he taught biology at Marlborough College before being ordained as a priest in the Church of England in 1963. He had four country parishes up to his retirement in 1992, and worked at the Crowhurst Home of Healing, Sussex between 1978 and 1984. He is still busy and his interests include cricket, natural history and ballet.

Peterson, Eugene H. Author of *The Message* (a contemporary Bible translation), he is Professor Emeritus of Spiritual Theology at Regent College, Vancouver, British Columbia. He served as a pastor for over 30 years and is a popular writer, poet and Bible teacher.

Piper, John (b. 1946) He has been senior pastor of Bethlehem Baptist Church in Minneapolis, Minnesota since 1980. He has written numerous books that 'call readers to spread a passion for the supremacy of God in all things for the joy of all peoples'. To read other poems that John has written, please visit http://desiringGOD.org.

Quarles, Francis (1592–1644) Supporter of the Royalist cause, he was a prolific poet. His *Emblems* was his century's most popular book.

Rossetti, Christina (1830–94) She was the sister of Dante Gabriel Rossetti, daughter of a noble Italian political exile. For much of her life she was an invalid.

Scott, Sir Walter (1771–1832) An Edinburgh-born novelist and poet who found inspiration in the Border country and Highlands of Scotland. He married the daughter of a French *émigré* and had a particular interest in ballad poetry. His publishing business foundered during the height of his immense popularity as a novelist.

Shaw, Luci (b. 1928) After a childhood in England, Australia and Canada, she took a degree at Wheaton College, near Chicago. She married Harold Shaw, now deceased, with whom she ran a publishing company. She has published many books of poetry, the latest of which is *The Angles of Light* (Shaw/Waterbrook, 2000). She remarried to John Hoyte in 1991.

Smart, Christopher (1722–71) He suffered severe mental illness and was confined in Bedlam (the Bethlehem Hospital), where he is thought to have written *Song to David* (see page 49).

Southwell, Robert (?1561–95) He was a Jesuit, educated at Douai and Rome. He wrote religious tracts, and was captured on his way to celebrate mass in 1592, and then tortured and executed.

Stone, Brian (d. 1995) Translator of several books of medieval verse and author of *Prisoner from Alamein* (1994). He was a founder member of the Open University, where he was Reader in Literature. His translation of 'The Ten Commandments' appears on p. 33.

Studdert Kennedy, Geoffrey Anketell (1883–1929) Affectionately nicknamed 'Woodbine Willie' by British troops (it referred to a brand of cigarettes he distributed), he was Chaplain to the Forces between 1916–19. An unconventional Church of England minister, he was appointed Rector of St Edmund, King and Martyr Church, Lombard Street, London.

Taylor, Edward (c. 1645–1729) A leading poet of New England, originally from Leicestershire, England. His manuscripts were not discovered until 1937, his *Poetical Works* being published 1939. He graduated from Harvard in 1671 and then was a minister in the frontier town of Westfield, Massachusetts until his death.

Tennyson, Alfred Lord (1809–92) Described as 'a supreme technician torn between the bardic voice and the solitary lyric', he was a prolific poet who in 1850 succeeded Wordsworth as Poet Laureate.

Tersteegen, Gerhard (1697–1769) A German Protestant devotional writer, whose pietism led him to retire into solitude, earning his living as a ribbon-weaver. He is known mainly for his hymns.

Updike, John (b. 1932) A major American novelist, who is also notable for his poetry and criticism. At one time he was on the staff of the *New Yorker* magazine.

Vaughan, Henry (1622?–95) A notable English poet of the Metaphysical period, who studied law and then became a medical practitioner in Brecknock and Newton-by-Usk. His publications of poems included *Silex Scintillans* (sacred poems).

Waltner-Toews, David (b. 1948) He is a lecturer at the University of Guelph, Canada; a veterinary epidemiologist specializing in zoonoses (diseases people share with other animals), ecosystem health, and international development; a poet; essayist; fiction writer; husband; father of two; and member of the Mennonite Church. His most recent poetry books are *The Impossible Uprooting* (McLelland & Stewart, 1995) and *The Fat Lady Struck Dumb* (Brick Books, 2000).

Warton, Thomas, the Elder (1688–1745) Poet, scholar, and father of Joseph Warton, critic and editor, and Thomas Warton the younger, poet and literary historian. A Fellow of Magdalen College, Oxford, he was Professor of Poetry from 1718 to 1728. Joseph prepared his father's *Poems on Several Occasions* (1748) for publication after his death.

Washbourne, Thomas (1606–87) Seventeenth-century cleric and author of *Divine Poems* (1654).

Watts, Isaac (1674–1748) He was a hymn-writer, Dissenting pastor and an eminent preacher. His hymns transformed worship in churches throughout England, with his influence spreading much wider.

Wesley, Charles (1707–88) The younger brother of John Wesley, he was a scholar, minister and hymn-writer, writing over 6,000 poems and hymns.

White, Henry Kirke (1785–1806) An English poet born in Nottingham. His publication in 1803 of *Clifton Grove* gained him the friendship of the Revd Charles Simeon of Cambridge, a leading Evangelical.

Wylie, Elinor (1885–1928) American poet and historical novelist, born in New Jersey. After her death her last husband, the poet William Rose Benét, edited her collected poems and prose, and wrote a brief study, *The Poetry and Prose of Elinor Wylie* (1934).

Zundel, Veronica (b.1953) She has been writing poetry for 30 years, and had poems published in several anthologies. She was the compiler of *Faith in her Words*, a collection of six centuries of women's poetry (Lion, 1991). She writes Bible reading notes for the Bible Reading Fellowship, and belongs to Britain's only Mennonite church.

INDEX OF POETS

INDEX OF TITLES

INDEX OF FIRST LINES